BUILDING THE HUMAN

BUILDING
THE HUMAN

Robert O. Johann

HERDER AND HERDER

1968
HERDER AND HERDER NEW YORK
232 Madison Avenue, New York 10016

Nihil obstat: Brendan W. Lawlor, Censor Librorum
Imprimatur: ✠ Robert F. Joyce, Bishop of Burlington
January 22, 1968

"The Nature of Philosophical Inquiry" was first published in the *Proceedings* of the American Catholic Philosophical Association, Washington, D.C., 1967; "Teilhard's Personalized Universe" was first published in the *Proceedings* of the 1964 Teilhard Conference held at Fordham University, New York; "Love and Reality" appeared as "Knowledge, Commitment, and the Real" in *Wisdom in Depth,* published by The Bruce Publishing Company, Milwaukee. All of the shorter pieces were first printed, occasionally under another title, in the pages of *America.*

Library of Congress Catalog Card Number: 68–20491
© 1968 by New American Library
Manufactured in the United States

Contents

Preface

THIS book brings together essays I have written during the past five years. They are philosophical essays in the sense that they are concerned with the bearing of what we believe and what we do on the over-all quality of our lives. Each essay attempts a critical evaluation of some current idea, habit or attitude in the light of how it works out in practice. Thus the aim is primarily practical, not theoretical. It is not to construct a philosophical system, but in a real sense to re-construct life itself. Any change in the particular beliefs that control our approach to life cannot but modify the shape of that life, the quality and texture of what we experience.

This explains the variety of topics touched upon. For "building the human" is not a matter of starting from scratch. It is really a question of rebuilding it, of rearranging and redirecting forces and energies already at work. The task of the philosopher is not to create something from nothing, but to search out existing obstacles to human growth and development, and to suggest ways of coping with them. This overriding concern for human growth is what unifies all our probings.

The essays that follow are grouped under three main headings. The basis for this arrangement is a certain understanding of what human growth is about—an understanding summed up in H. Richard Niebuhr's image of man-the-responder. Niebuhr's point is that man's development does not consist in the progressive realization of predetermined goals. Nor is it a matter of conforming one's life to laws that descend from on high. Life, for Niebuhr, is the very process of interaction between man and the world, that inclusive and continuing dialogue whose emergent meaning depends on how intelligently man responds to the forces acting upon him.

From this point of view, human fulfillment is radically this-worldly. It does not lie somewhere beyond the boundaries of everyday life but must be sought within its confines. It consists in the integrity, harmony, coherence—what we might call the esthetic quality—of the very process which is life. Since this quality of life depends on what man does, on the way he actively inter-venes in his environment, and since the appropriateness of his interventions is a function of the adequacy of his ideas, the in-dispensable role of thought in the enhancement of life's quality is manifest. Thinking is not simply for the contemplation of life as something already complete; it enters into the very making of life. By empirically discriminating and correlating the factors that have a bearing on its concrete shape, thoughtful inquiry aids in trans-forming human experience from a haphazard and irrational affair into one whose inherent possibilities are progressively capable of conscious realization.

This crucial role of *thought* in humanizing life makes it impera-tive at the outset that we avoid any misconceptions in its regard. The mind is not a passive spectator but an active participant in world process. Hence Part One of the book is devoted to stressing this operational and creative nature of intellectual inquiry.

Inquiry so understood, however, is meaningful only in a *situa-tion* that is really open to intelligent transformation. If the world is conceived as a closed network of systematic relationships there is no room for intellect. Indeed, there would be nothing for man to do. Real action would be impossible. Part Two, therefore, emphasizes the open and indeterminate character of the situation in which we find ourselves. In contrast to some more traditional views, the picture that emerges is one of the world as on-going event. It is a world that is inherently unfinished, one whose human sense is not antecedent and original, but consequent upon man's intervention.

How, then, should man intervene? What dispositions of mind and heart must he bring to his task if there is to be any chance of success? If human sense is not something given but something to be achieved, then everything hangs on the sort of *response* man makes to the challenge confronting him. Some of the features of the response that seems called for are explored in Part Three.

Each of the three parts begins with a selection of shorter essays touching on various aspects of the theme under consideration. These short essays first appeared in the pages of *America* magazine, but they were also written with the needs of this book in mind. They represent an attempt (which many readers of *America* seem to have found helpful) to probe a specific problem and open it up for further reflection and inquiry. Though each short essay can stand by itself, the problem it takes up is nonetheless related to the larger problem of the section to which it belongs. This larger problem receives explicit attention in one or more longer essays concluding each part. These are philosophically more technical but they do not pretend, any more than the shorter ones, to say the last word. Their aim is simply to explore in greater depth and detail the implications of the over-all theme of the section.

One final word. A work of philosophy, like a work of literature, is inevitably autobiographical. In the selection of topics, personal bias is always at work. If a reader wonders why other contemporary problems have been neglected in favor of the ones actually treated, my answer is simply that these are the ones in the past five years that have preoccupied me. Although I have not touched all the bases, I trust there are readers with like concerns who may find these pages helpful.

R.O.J.

PART ONE

THOUGHT

Of all human enterprises, philosophical inquiry is the most practical. It is the use of intelligence to liberalize action, to open up new possibilities.

Philosophy is also passionate. It is spurred by dissatisfaction with what needs correction, zeal in the communal search for greater sense, joy at new harmonies achieved. It is mind in the service of heart, a discipline in the service of human growth.

Philosophical inquiry is, at its best, an adventure in making life whole.

I.

Why Philosophy?

In our age of streamlined efficiency, philosophy is under a cloud. Students, unsure of themselves and looking for a clear guide to life, are impatient with the endless bickerings of the different schools of thought. And men of affairs, when they consult philosophers for light on important human issues, ordinarily find themselves more perplexed at the end of their discussions than they were at the start. It may not be out of place, therefore, to say a few words in philosophy's defense.

Disenchantment with philosophy usually results from a misunderstanding of its nature and function. It is compared unfavorably with the sciences, when really its aims and scope are quite different. A brief look at man's predicament will show what I mean.

Man experiences his own life as a problem. His very capacity to think, to step back from his immediate dealings and plan his future, dissolves those bonds of necessity by which everything else is governed and puts his own life in his hands.

Man's thinking lifts him out of the snug realm of nature where things proceed as a matter of course. It makes him a person weighed down by the need to decide. Man is a being who must himself determine what he will do with his life, how he will relate himself to all that surrounds him. He is literally compelled by his freedom to take a personal stand on everything and be responsible for the stand he takes. Philosophy is simply his effort to avoid doing this in the dark.

Since the purpose of philosophy is thus to throw some light on the meaning of life as a whole, to give man some idea of what he is about and what is at stake in the particular decisions he makes, the apparent limitations and failures of philosophy become more understandable. For human life is not something finished and complete that can be studied apart from the person who lives it. Life is a task in which the thinker himself is involved, and its texture and quality depend on his own free response.

Small wonder then that philosophers disagree among themselves, and that the work of one cannot be simply appropriated by the next. Since what a philosopher studies is something to which his own freedom contributes, no purely objective test of his findings is possible. He can be guided and helped by the thought of others—the importance of a philosophic tradition cannot be overestimated—but the truth of what is said philosophically he must ultimately judge for himself.

Yet, despite its inherent limitations, the philosophic enterprise is one that cannot be dispensed with. If the nature of its task prevents philosophy from achieving the kind of public success that science enjoys, still nothing is more intimate to each of us than the reality it tries to explore—and through its exploration to shape.

As the French philosopher Blondel once observed, philosophy is not to explain life but to help constitute it. By making man aware of the implications of his actions, of the range and scope of his life, it lifts that life to a level that cannot be otherwise reached. It is a level on which man is faced not with the disposition of things or the mastery of the world that surrounds him, but with the disposition of himself and the decisions that determine his own meaning. If on this level he finds no ready-made answers that can be grasped independently of his personal commitments and the experience to which they give rise, it is nevertheless no slight service of philosophy to make him aware even of that.

Ultimate Meaning

Not too long ago, Daniel Callahan summed up the modern temper, even of most Catholics, when he suggested that the time has come to set aside our metaphysical worries about final goals and ultimate meanings, and focus our attention on the immediate issue of shaping the world in which we live. We should concentrate, he says, on the natural and social sciences, and let go the traditional philosophic quest for total vision if we want to catch up with our world.

The suggestion has the merit of being direct and straight-forward. Because it misinterprets the alternatives confronting us, however, it is also dangerously misleading. For our choice is not between the ultimate meanings of philosophy and the more immediate, practical meanings of science, but between two conceptions of ultimacy. To fail to recognize this is to court confusion if not outright disaster.

Actually, the root of the problem lies in the fact that, for many people, the idea of "ultimate meaning" is tied up with the realm of the "really real," a realm lying somewhere behind or above our ordinary experience and supplying it with a value and sense it does not have of itself. Philosophy's quest for ultimate meaning becomes then a quest for this Super Reality, in comparison with which ordinary events are felt to lack solidity. In Pieper's terminology, its aim is "to step beyond the sectional, partial environment of the workaday world into a position face to face with the Whole." Small wonder then that, for the growing number of people who are not interested in stepping out of this world but, on the contrary, feel called to involve themselves ever more deeply and passionately in it, philosophy becomes an irrelevant distraction. If they turn their backs on philosophy, it is because philosophy has first turned its back on their world.

But the words "ultimate meaning" can be used in a different sense. They need not imply some invidious contrast between the "really real" and the common concerns of men. If the word "meaning" signifies in general "potentiality for consequences," then clearly we can distinguish two levels of consequences—a distinction that corresponds roughly to that between the sciences and the humanities—without ever having to take our feet off the ground.

First of all, objects discriminated in our experience may be conceptually linked together in terms of their dynamic connections with one another. They may be understood as serially interrelated phases in an ordered process of change. The exploration of such connections is fundamentally the concern of science. Secondly, however, the meaning of such objects may be sought not simply in terms of their connections with one another, but in the bearing they have, their potentiality for consequences, on the quality, sense and style of human life itself. It is the search for this sort of meaning that characterizes the humanities (including, especially, philosophy). These ulterior humanistic meanings are ignored when we deal with things "scientifically," and quite properly so, since such final meanings are capable of control only when a sequential order of changes has first of all been determined. Yet although ignored by science, they cannot be ignored altogether if science itself is not to be dehumanized. For only in the measure that we critically explore the connection between what we do and the way we deal with things, on the one hand, and what we undergo, the humanity (or lack of it) of our lives, on the other, do the possibilities for control opened up by science become humanly fruitful.

The bearing, then, of all our beliefs and practices (including the possibilities that science discloses) on the human sense of our lives is the sort of ultimate meaning that genuine philosophy pursues. Philosophy has to determine, as Dewey put it, "the place of science in life, the place of its peculiar subject matter in the wide scheme of materials we experience" if science itself is "to contribute to the life of humanity." Exclusive preoccupation with science results not only in ignoring its vital context but also in leaving the determination of what to do with all the facts amassed by science to the haphazard and amateur kind of philosophizing that the man in the street and (too often) the contemporary critic of philosophy engage in.

Philosophy, to be sure, cannot by itself solve the problem of life. Philosophy is reflection, and apart from action, reflection— even on ultimate meanings—modifies nothing and hence resolves nothing. But as Dewey also notes—and our "new" pragmatists would do well to study him—"In a complicated and perverse world, action which is not informed with vision, imagination and reflection [and here Dewey means philosophy] is more likely to increase confusion and conflict than to straighten things out."

Thought, Feeling and Reality

Contemporary man sometimes seems to have lost his capacity for joy. It is almost as if he were bent on making himself insensitive to the consummatory in experience, as if he were determined to develop a kind of trained incapacity for happiness.

Dewey once remarked that science was able to advance only when men became "willing to turn away from precious possessions, willing to let drop what they own" in the matter of immediate ends and enjoyments, in order to concentrate on the relational aspects of things, on means and instrumentalities. The danger today is that the instrumental is becoming coterminous with the real; that the world turns into a conglomeration of means without ends; that the withdrawal from the immediate, which was meant to be provisional and for its enhancement, becomes final; that the really precious possessions are not only dropped temporarily but are lost permanently.

The root of the difficulty lies in a faulty conception of the relationships between thought, feeling and reality. Thought, in the form of scientific inquiry, has been taken as providing us access to the truly real. As science has developed, its objects have become progressively more remote from the things and affairs of everyday life. The scientific object is notoriously stripped of all those qualities for which things are prized in direct experience. It becomes a matter of mathematical and mechanistic relations, devoid of everything that makes for love and appreciation.

The result has been to introduce an unbridgeable chasm between feeling and reality. Feelings become completely private and subjective. They belong to the realm of appearance, not to that of things as they are. For if the proper object of science is a mathematico-mechanical world and if the object of science defines true and perfect reality, then the objects of love, appreciation and devotion cannot be included within true reality. They become simply private impressions without objective import.

The trouble with all this is that it turns the world upside down. Man's thematically cognitive relationship with the real is neither original nor final. It is essentially transitional, mediating between objects of direct appreciation that are casual in their occurrence and those that are intelligently regulated. Scientific knowledge is not a union with the real as distinct from the merely apparent. By turning from things in their immediacy to view them in their relationships and efficacies, it provides us not with new reality but with new and effective ways of intending and dealing with what is already at hand. And what is at hand *is* the real. Reality, far from being something behind or under direct experience, is precisely the ongoing, inclusive affair of everyday life, whose immediate quality, as something open to improvement, is the beginning and end of all inquiry. The point of science is not to provide a substitute for this experience, but to bring it under control.

This brings us back to the matter of feeling. Feelings are not arbitrary, isolated occurrences taking place under our skins. They are the pervasive and unifying qualities of the interactive process between person and environment that is human life itself. Instead of being irrelevant to what is going on, they are its culminating sense—the sense of that inclusive transaction which is my life, at any stage in its development. Thus restlessness and dissatisfaction are not simply private and subjective events, but the actualized character of a developing situation that is troubled and unsatisfactory. By the same token, joy is not a mere inner

19

and irrelevant accompaniment of some particular, objective relationship. It is itself the objective sense of the relationship in its completeness and self-sufficiency. Dissatisfaction is a situation characterized by need—the need for inquiry and correction. Joy is a situation characterized by wholeness. It is the real as consummatory and, to that extent, self-justifying.

In relation, then, to reality, feelings are far from frivolous distractions. Instead, they are the ultimate qualitative differences in that inclusive transaction which is reality. Since these differences are the cumulative effect of all the factors involved in the transaction, their regulation presupposes an awareness of such factors in their bearing on the outcome. But the outcome is what is important. To suppress feeling is to deprive knowledge of its point. To be afraid of feeling is to be afraid of finalities, of ever getting anywhere; it is to be always on the way. To become incapable of direct appreciation and enjoyment is to make that way endless. For the joy of immediate experience is and remains the end. Forgetting that, we forget what life is for and about.

Reflective Pragmatism

An increasing number of Christian thinkers are turning to American philosophy for insight and inspiration. They see in the pragmatism of James, Peirce and Dewey not only a general program for liberating intelligence in the service of life, but more specifically, an approach to meaning and truth that offers exciting possibilities for the reinterpretation of religion. The task facing such thinkers, however, is a huge one. Besides the usual struggle of innovators—

especially in religious matters—to win a hearing for their ideas, they have the added difficulty of distinguishing their approach from the abortive pragmatism already so characteristic of modern man.

The distrust of speculative thought in our age is notorious. There is less and less concern with the larger issues of human life and destiny, and more and more with the specific problems thrust on us by modern technology. The attempt to deal with these problems has disclosed the utter inadequacy of relying on inherited ideas and preconceptions formed without regard for the novel context in which they must now take effect. The *a priori* approach to concrete issues has been dropped in favor of the methods of science itself. The isolation of particular problems, the determination of the precise conditions on which their resolution depends, the exclusion from view of all data and considerations that are not immediately relevant, the acceptance of ideas solely on the basis of their operational effectiveness—these and like procedures have become the order of the day.

We are thus developing a breed of men whose whole loyalty is not to "some passionately held philosophy of life" but "simply to the job at hand, to good workmanship." Limited objectives have taken the place of absolute goals, and "here and now" workable solutions, the position once held by final salvation. The pragmatists are taking over.

But if we are clearly undergoing what one writer has called a "massive cultural shift" in our beliefs and valuation, a kind of inner revolution, we are also—and with good reason—increasingly worried about its outcome. The pragmatism of modern man has, so far, disrupted life more than it has promoted its values. By viewing life as a set of distinct problems that can be approached piecemeal, instead of as a continuous and comprehensive process

21

all of whose aspects are mutually interdependent, modern man has only succeeded in putting it out of joint. Far from enhancing the world, he has come close to making it uninhabitable.

These manifest defects of the pragmatism currently practiced make many people uneasy about extending its influence. But the point I wish to make is that they result not from the doctrine itself, but from the short-sighted and abortive way it has been applied.

The central conviction of pragmatism is that the ideas and principles by which life is to be shaped have their origin and final test in the experiential process itself. Real knowledge is a matter of the perceived consequences of our active dealings with our surroundings. Independent of such consequences, all our ideas and interpretations are necessarily provisional, hypotheses still to be tested. From this point of view, truth is not something we first arrive at by purely "mental" means and then try to live. Nor is knowledge the possession of some stable order beyond experience and in accord with which experience itself should be moulded. Rather, truly to know is to possess ways of acting in concert with others that, in relation to envisioned goals, on-going practice shows to be reliable. We come to the truth only in and through the very process of living.

If this is so, then there is nothing in pragmatism to prevent its advocates from concerning themselves with the quality and coherence of human life as a whole. A pragmatist need not, as the modern variety inclines to do, break up life into a series of separate problems to the complete neglect of its over-all sense. Indeed, precisely by pragmatic standards, the disruptive consequences of such an approach are proof of its inadequacy. Regarding over-all views, the only thing that pragmatism excludes is their elaboration and retention regardless of their practical consequences.

For the pragmatist, all intellectual products are tools in life's service. They have value only as they are instrumental in the achievement of concrete sense—i.e., the integration of the life process itself in such a way that *all* its elements complement and reinforce one another. Such comprehensive integration is the real goal of pragmatism and its justification as a style of thought. This is what today's unreflective pragmatists too often forget. It is not that they are too pragmatic; they are not pragmatic enough.

Faith and Philosophy

Can a Catholic really be a philosopher? Many people say no. A philosopher is one who raises ultimate questions. A Catholic is one who by faith already knows the answers. If you put the two together, you have either a believer who does not really believe or a thinker who does not really think. Or so the objection goes.

The objection is not to be taken lightly, as anyone who tries to be both a Catholic and a philosopher soon comes to realize. His co-religionists are often suspicious of his "rationalism." At best, they feel he is wasting his time. Why bother with philosophy when the faith itself has the answers to eternal life? On the other hand, his non-Catholic colleagues are doubtful of his freedom to follow the evidence wherever it leads. If he is a Catholic, his mind is already closed. The first tend to question his faith; the second, his integrity.

The difficulty is an old one. And part of it, at least, stems from the kinds of solution that often are put forward to meet it. For example, philosophy is sometimes supposed to be a matter of

23

"pure reason" (as opposed to theology, which proceeds in the light of faith). The Catholic philosopher, therefore, is one who, in his work at least, suspends his belief or prescinds from it. He tries to operate in the light of reason alone and see how things look from a purely "natural" point of view.

The only trouble with this is that it does not work. For philosophy is not something that "reason" does, but is something that *I* do, I who am a Catholic—who am already committed to Christ and His Church; whose experience, the subject-matter of my reflection, is already structured, ordered, transformed by what I believe. "Reason" is not some kind of neutral observer to whom I go to find out how things are, independently of faith. The "reason" in question is *my* reason; it is myself as capable of reflection. And what I have to reflect upon is not some world-in-itself; it is precisely *my experience* of the world, an experience that my free commitments (most especially my faith) have shaped from the inside. What then is going on? How is what I do not theology?

It seems to me that anyone who is a Catholic has a double work of reflection to perform. Like anyone else who is serious about what he does, he must try to think out the implications of his life so that his actions may proceed from as complete an awareness as possible of what is at stake in them. But since his life, as a Catholic, is a life of response to the God of revelation, his thinking must go in two directions at once.

First, he must think about what God has revealed and about the invitation He offers. This is an effort to grasp reflectively the whole of revelation in its integrity and coherence, and to fathom its meaning. It is a work of reflection whose subject matter is the integral word of God and whose norm is the living

24

magisterium of the Church, to whom that word has been confided. It is theology.

If, however, we look upon the life of faith, not now in terms of that to which it is a response, but precisely as a response that *I* make and that I, as a free individual, am answerable for, then the need for another work of reflection becomes manifest. For my responsibility before God for whatever I do can never be suspended, and is not suspended here. If I believe, I remain responsible before God for my belief, responsible for adhering to Him in this precise fashion, responsible for accepting what proclaims itself to be His Church as really being His Church, responsible for my judgment that, despite the honest objections of so many contemporary thinkers, my believing is in no way opposed to my essential vocation as a person, but actually promotes it; that it does not corrupt my relations with the world and with men, but perfects them.

In other words, I as an individual, relying on my own powers of discernment and unable to place responsibility for my actions on anybody's shoulders but my own, must be able to judge that the very life of faith is a responsible way for a human being to behave. To make this judgment, however, at least to make it explicitly, requires a reflective effort that is directed on the whole structure of human experience, on the exigencies of personal life, and on the demands and import of the faith, seen not in terms of itself merely, but as *part of experience*. And such a reflective effort is, precisely, philosophy.

The Catholic philosopher, therefore, neither prescinds from his faith nor theologizes. Like any other philosopher, he turns his reflection on the totality of his experience and tries to see for himself—and make intelligible to others—how everything in it, including his deepest commitments, forms a consistent whole.

Reason, Nature and Morality

An editorial in the *Catholic Mind* once called attention to the fact that the controversy over the morality of contraceptive practices has widened into a dispute about the nature of morality as such. At issue in the dispute is the very idea of natural law. But the disputants are not neatly divided, as the editorial would seem to suggest, into defenders and opponents of natural-law morality. It is not a question of simply holding on to the concept of natural law or of abandoning it altogether. More profoundly, at least within Catholic circles, the discussion centers on the precise meaning to be assigned to it.

That the notion of natural law needs careful interpretation if it is not to be misleading is suggested by the following remark of Père de Finance. In the section of his *Essai sur l'agir humain* that treats of the essence of moral value, he writes: "It is not because reason is natural that we should follow reason; on the contrary, it is only because our nature shares in reason that it is good to act in accord with our nature." The remark is crucial. It is not nature as such that has moral relevance; it is reason. The morally good is not simply what is in accord with nature, but what presents itself as reasonable in the particular circumstances. The eminent dignity of human nature, Père de Finance continues, springs from its aptitude to follow reason, to determine itself reasonably; only in terms of this capacity does it have moral value.

From even this much, one can see the at least questionable validity of arguments that immediately draw moral conclusions from the determinate characteristics of natural processes. If Père de Finance is right, then the fact that a person interferes with or disturbs a particular physical process is *by itself* morally irrelevant. The only question is whether or not, in a given case, it is reasonable for him to do so. That it may indeed be reasonable, however, presupposes a different conception of reason's role in moral affairs than the one all too frequently assigned to it.

In conventional presentations of natural-law theory, reason is given a largely passive role. Its only function is to take note of man's natural constitution, the determinate and hierarchical complex of his needs and fulfillments, and to present this to the will as the pattern to be followed. It adds nothing of its own to nature besides awareness—the reflective awareness of an order already constituted. From this point of view, being reasonable means conforming to the known patterns of nature. Following reason means determining oneself in accord with the natural structures disclosed to reason.

Such, however, is not the only possible view of reason's role. Indeed, according to Père de Finance, unless one moves farther than this, one has not even reached the moral order. For the moral order is grounded, not in determinate nature, but in reason's openness to the Absolute. Through reason, man is open to Being itself, aware not merely of facts but of possibilities, and, in the light of these possibilities, called to the continual enhancement of the determinate situations in which he finds himself.

Human nature, properly speaking, is not something complete and self-enclosed, a detailed map for guiding our conduct. Human nature is a task, a project of promotion, a work of love. It is reason responding to the Infinite in, through and beyond the finite. Correspondingly, reason's role is not simply to record but, in the light of Being, to innovate. Its vocation is not merely to register natural data, but to judge and transform them in the light of its own Ideal. (Think, for example, of the persevering inventiveness required for the achievement of a just society in a constantly changing world.) Instead of being true to nature, therefore, as something fixed and settled, standing over against it, reason's task is to be true to itself. The morally right is not what conforms to determinate nature but what conforms to the dictates of a reason enlisted in love's service. From this point of view, being reasonable means precisely acting in accord with reason's recommendations—a reason open to the Absolute and inspired by love.

Criticism, then, of conventional natural-law arguments does not necessarily spring from a subjectivistic bias, personalist or otherwise, or from some sort of anti-rational and relativistic confusion. Its origin is not a desire to extol personal freedom over nature but a refusal, on the contrary, to exalt brute, natural facticity over man's capacity to cope with it rationally. Instead of ousting reason, many critics of the "natural law" are seeking simply to restore it to its central and creative role. They recall that for Aquinas himself the nature that is morality's norm is not a complex of impersonal structures but precisely *recta ratio* —reason rectified by love. And they think it might not be a bad idea to get back to this liberating and refreshing view.

Intelligence and Values

It is fashionable nowadays to disparage the role of intellect in determining ultimate goals. Because the realm of value lies outside the scope of scientific methodology, it is thought to lie beyond the reach of intelligence, as well. Final objectives become matters of personal preference. Thus Peirce can write: "In regard to the greatest affairs of life, the wise man follows his heart and does not trust his head. This should be the method of every man, no matter how powerful his intellect."

There is merit in the admonition. The good is not immediately the term of thought, but of feeling and sensibility. It is not disclosed by a process of dispassionate inquiry, but only through the stresses and strains of personal involvement. The good is what we lack when we are sad and have when we are glad. It causes us worry when it is threatened, outrage when it is violated, grief when it fades and disappears. The good is what is experienced as congenial, healing, fulfilling, worth fighting and struggling for. It never comes merely as the answer to a question; it is always the answer to a prayer.

The role of the heart in disclosing the good is undeniable. If we did not experience our own being in terms of desires and aspirations, we would never be aware of anything at all as good. Granting, however, that the heart thus lights up the realm of value, we must still ask whether its promptings by themselves are reliable guides. Are "reasons of the heart" reasons enough for what we do? To think of the pathetic, often destructive, choices they have been called on to justify is already to begin to doubt it.

The difficulty with following the heart is that it leads in different directions at the same time. Although it illuminates the whole range of values, it does so indiscriminately. If by "heart" we mean the dynamic structure of man, his affective accord with all that is naturally congenial, then we must say that the heart is a bundle of distinct and often conflicting drives. Some urge a man toward whatever is necessary for his well-being as an individual organism. Others, on a deeper level, impel him to look for his completion and a deepening of self-awareness through association and union with his fellows. Most profound, however, and completely transforming these prior dynamisms, is man's affective kinship with Being itself, which calls him continually to live in its light and be bent on promoting its reign. The realm of goods lighted up by man's inclinations is thus all but chaotic in its diversity. The ease and comfort of material abundance, the security of social acceptance, the gracious support of friendship, the healing intimacy of conjugal love, the delight in order and rationality, the exhilaration of creativity, the abiding consolation of God's enveloping presence and the peace that comes in His service—all these are terms of the heart's hankerings. Unless they are sorted out and integrated in a total quest, their separate tuggings can tear the heart apart.

What is needed, therefore, is first a work of intelligent discernment. Man's manifold aims must be distinguished from one another and then grasped in their interconnectedness. A hierarchy must be established on the basis of objective importance. What counts here is not the mere force of feeling, but how it is interpreted; not the brute tug of a particular good, but the meaning it has for our total being. In animals, this ordering of drives is instinctive; with man, only persistent reflection combined with docility to its findings can bring it about.

Docility to the findings of intellect, however, means keeping them steadily in view. Besides discernment, there is need for recollection. For the heat of action tends to distract us from everything except the immediate goal. We become hypnotized by the particular, caught up in its vicissitudes, and, with our attention thus monopolized, fluctuate between extremes of joy and sadness that are out of all proportion to their occasions. Recollection, on the other hand, enables us to bring all our separate strivings into the ultimate orbit of the soul's relation to God. As Jean Guitton observes, the recollected man is able to extract even from his troubles a mysterious increase of being, whereas the most intense pleasure, if it is not assumed by the spirit, leaves us restless and empty. Failure to stand in God's presence corrupts everything. For those who are mindful of Him, however, even frustration can contribute to growth.

The intellect's final service to the heart is one of purifying criticism. For the most dedicated person is still open to confusing his isolated interests with the cause of Being itself. Only unremitting self-criticism can insure that our efforts to promote Being do not degenerate into flurries of self-seeking and that earnestly pursued "reforms" do not become forms of evasion.

In the human enterprise, therefore, head and heart are natural allies, and neither can go it alone. The heart supplies energy and push for the undertaking, but its happy outcome depends on using the head.

The Future of Philosophy

How relate the individual free subject to the rest of reality? According to Erich Fromm, this is the basic problem facing philosophers today. Just as psychological maturity is reached only when a person, after emerging as an individual from his surroundings, freely enters into a responsible relationship with them, so too, philosophical maturity demands, besides the distinction between "subjectivity" and "objectivity," their intelligible unification.

Contemporary man is too anxiously aware of his own selfhood ever to be happy again with "objective" philosophies that ignore it. But the barrenness of theories ignoring everything else is also coming home to him. If, as he sees it, pure objectivity is illusory, he is also learning that pure subjectivity is a bore. What he wants is a way of understanding himself as a significantly free initiative involved in a meaningful (not absurd!) world.

A first step toward such understanding is a conception of the world that leaves room for individual initiative. The world cannot be one that, prior to human intervention, already makes complete sense. In a closed network of wholesale, systematic relationships, selfhood is meaningless. The self can fit into such a scheme, not as a self, but only as a member of a class. What is needed, instead, is a view of the world as ongoing event, "an affair of affairs" (Dewey), more a matter of dramatic encounters than of logical connections, of novel occasions than of fixed and settled routines.

e. e. cummings once wrote of "the gay great happening illimitably earth." The word "happening" is just right. The world is a *happening*. Its sense is not something antecedent and original. It issues from the interplay of an endless variety of factors and forces, one of which is human intelligence. It is an emergent sense in whose shaping both intellect and initiative can have a part.

This brings up the second prerequisite for the desired synthesis. It is a conception of intelligence as essentially practical and creative, more a participant in world process than a disinterested bystander, more esthetic in its basic orientation and functioning than simply scientific, more bent on *making* sense where it is not (yet!) than on complacently presuming its presence or despairingly bemoaning its lack. Because of his presumption of wholesale antecedent sense, the objectivist is reduced to the role of spectator. Because he craves such sense but does not find it, the subjectivist withdraws his concern from an "absurd" world to fix it on himself. And today's hero, the scientist, because *his* concern is facts and not values, finds himself with a whole arsenal of means with no way of deciding how to use them. In their different ways, all ignore the primary role of intelligence, which, able to discriminate between the fitting and the discrepant, is called to intervene constantly in the ongoing course of events in favor of ever greater coherence and concrete reasonableness. Science, to be sure, is essential in this enterprise. Effective intervention presupposes a knowledge of what is connected with what. But the determination of continually more inclusive and humanly satisfying goals, of what makes for life's enhancement and what does not—this is a matter of esthetic judgment, which only use can develop.

Finally, there is the need to recognize the transcendent ground of personal initiative and responsibility. Unless a person is related in action to more than the particularities that successively preoccupy him, his life as a whole can never make sense. He may, of course, arbitrarily select a goal to which he subordinates everything else. He can thus impose a kind of unity on his life. But the price of such unification is the cultivated inability to respond to each separate occasion on its own merits. Plural encounters can coalesce into a meaningful *life,* without the loss or suppression of their distinctive qualities, only if each is also a phase in a single, continuing encounter—i.e., only if there is One whom a person encounters in all his encounters and answers in all his actions. Only in the context of transcendence can the bits and pieces of man's life be simply and wonderfully what they are, and still add up. Only in relation to God is man freed from the need, in his search for coherence, to force a sense on things that they do not have.

The world as ongoing event, intellect as esthetic agent, and the human person as rooted in transcendence—these three ideas do not, to be sure, constitute the self-understanding that contemporary man seeks. But they may help him toward it.

II.

The Nature of Philosophical Inquiry

IN his article on the starting-point of philosophical reflection, Maurice Blondel calls attention to the difficulty of combining the universal scope of such reflection with technical and methodological precision.

There is, as it were, a kind of conflict between the matter and form of philosophy. On the one hand, philosophy has traditionally pretended to exercise a kind of universal jurisdiction and to find its matter in the general movement of mankind's spiritual life, in those problems and questions whose resolution concerns us all. On the other hand, philosophical reflection seems unable to make headway except at the price of progressive specialization and self-limitation. The various techniques of approach and treatment that have been developed have had the effect of splintering the philosophic enterprise into different camps of specialists who give the impression of being out of touch not only with the common life of humanity but with one another as well. Whereas the special sciences have elaborated a kind of universal method for handling their several distinct and limited areas, a method which makes possible not only communication between them but a cumulative and collective progress as well, philosophers seem bent on adapting the universal object of their discipline to a whole range of special

35

methodologies which seem more indicative of individual biases and points of view than of any requirements of subject-matter.

This split between form and matter has never been more manifest than it is today. As John Macmurray points out, there is a growing consensus that philosophy cannot solve its old problems with its old methods. But here the consensus ends. When it comes to interpreting it, two divergent paths open up. On the one hand, we have those who discard the problems to concentrate on perfecting a method, and on the other, those who relinquish method to be free to wrestle with problems. The first make the problem of philosophy primarily a problem of form and methodology, and end up with a minimum of substance. The second, moved by the poignancy of substantive issues and finding "no formal analysis that is adequate to the task . . ." set scientific form aside and, in Macmurray's words, "wallow in metaphor and suggestion." The net effect is to leave the human enterprise at large without rational guidance. Reason turns in on itself and life muddles along. The only thing is, such muddling is today a luxury we can ill afford. We are literally at a crossroads and life itself is at stake.

One cannot probe with any depth into the real nature of philosophical inquiry without developing along the way a fairly definite view of human life as a whole. Since the nature of philosophical inquiry is itself a philosophical issue, any adequate determination of it will itself imply a whole philosophy. The position elaborated here is no exception. It may be well, therefore, even if it is impossible here to justify it fully, at least to indicate the general position from which I am operating. This position, for want of a better name, can be called *ontological pragmatism*. It is a kind of pragmatism, since it views thematic knowledge as an instrumental function of experience aimed at the latter's transformation. Ideas must be tested by consequences, by what occurs when they are acted upon. Their validity is measured by their success, when used as directives, in making experience itself more richly meaningful and coherent. On the other hand, we call our position an *ontological* pragmatism, since we contend that this instrumental conception of knowing, far from implying a veil between us and reality, actually enables us progressively to discern its nature. If this is true in general, it is no less so when applied to answering the question: What is philosophy? The validity of a conception of philosophy's nature must be tested by what it leads to in practice. Any conception that blocks the forward movement of experience, that is less fruitful than some alternative in promoting concrete coherence and reasonableness, can hardly be said to be in greater correspondence with, or more in tune with, reality than its rival. The warrant for the particular hypothesis which I shall suggest about the nature of philosophical enquiry can only be its greater potential, when put into practice, for the enrichment of experience.

In order to give some order to what follows, I shall first say something about the nature of inquiry in general. Secondly, I shall take up the matter of context—the cultural, communal context of all our inquiries. Here I shall try to specify the sort of perplexity to which philosophy, as a distinctive kind of inquiry, is a response. Finally, I shall indicate briefly three distinct but inseparable phases of philosophy's effort to resolve this perplexity. These three phases I shall term *logic, phenomenology,* and *meta-pragmatics.*

1. *The nature of inquiry in general.* Inquiry may be provisionally defined as man's effort to integrate his experience as

responsible agent. For this to be understood, a word must first be said about how we are using the term "experience." "Experience" here will signify the interactive process itself interior to which the human self is in dynamic relation with the whole range of the other. In this sense, experience is not something going on within the self, something private and subjective. It envelopes the other no less than the self in a kind of totality that is all-inclusive. Nothing can be conceived as outside of or utterly divorced from this process.

Within this process, man functions as the *responder*. This notion of "responder" has its roots in that objective awareness, that presence to the other as other, that is characteristic of man. Unlike the brute animal which "lives, as it were, ecstatically immersed in its environment which it carries along as a snail carries its shell," man finds himself standing over against the environment with which he is in interaction. Hence his actions are never simply reactions to stimuli but are, in H. Richard Niebuhr's phrase, "answers to actions upon him," answers which must fit into the ongoing process like statements in a dialogue and which, as a consequence, not only look backwards to what has been "said" but are made in anticipation of a reply, that is, of "objections, confirmations and corrections."

Human action, therefore, always presupposes an interpretation of what is going on and of what may be expected as its consequence. The human agent is aware that the future hangs on the present, that what he will undergo depends in no small measure on what he does, on the adequacy of his response. By the same token, he is aware of the complex and inclusive situation in which he finds himself as a question being addressed to him. It may, indeed, be a familiar question, one for which he feels he has the answer from having met and coped with it

38

before. On the other hand, it may have novel features which call into question the adequacy of past habits for dealing with it and give rise to hesitancy and uncertainty.

This uncertainty, it should be noted, is not something private and subjective. It is not something simply in the mind of the agent. Nor is it merely something negative, a sheer absence of knowledge. On the contrary, it is a positive and pervasive quality of the interactive process itself, of the inclusive situation embracing agent *and* environment and which may be described as one of tension, discord, discrepancy. There is a positive incoherence between environmental demands and the agent's habitual equipment to meet them. And it is this incoherence that calls forth inquiry.

From this point of view, inquiry is what the agent does, the operations he performs, to remove this tension and incoherence, to transform the objectively unsettled state of affairs into one that is settled, to reintegrate his experience as responsible agent so that the quality of discord that marked it may be replaced by one of harmony. This will be the case when the question raised by the environment's actions on him once more becomes a familiar question; when he has acquired a new and reliable way (or *habit*) for dealing with it. Needless to say, the achievement of such a habit presupposes that whatever estimate he forms of what is required of him be put to the test of practice. Prior to such testing, that is, prior to acting upon the newly formed interpretation of what is called for and noting the confirmations or correctness it receives in the process, the interpretation itself remains merely a hunch or hypothesis whose reliability is not assured. In other words, the relationship between man the responder and that which demands his response is still unsettled. A kind of wariness and probing are still in order. The process of inquiry is not yet concluded. Thus we may say that inquiry in its full and proper sense is not merely a matter of reflection, of taking thought, of forming a preliminary estimate or interpretation, but also includes those operations and dealings with the other by which alone the estimate can be established as warranted. Only when the agent is newly equipped with a habit on which he can count is he once more *at home* in his surroundings.

If this is so, then inquiry may be defined as that whole process by which man's experience of himself as responder to actions on him is transformed from an incoherent state to one whose elements hang together, from a state of tension and discord to one that is resolved and integrated. Inquiry thus mediates between two states of affairs that are immediately and qualitatively distinct and that of themselves respectively provoke and terminate it. One does not have to inquire as to whether inquiry is called for. The objective discrepancy between past habit and novel circumstances presents itself immediately to the wary, responsible agent as calling for it. He may, indeed, decide to ignore the call, to plunge into action without forethought, without first attempting to resolve the discrepancy, hoping the meanwhile not to be too severely chastened by subsequent experience —the very urgency of the demand for action will at times preclude anything else—but the unsatisfactoriness of proceeding in this fashion, even when he has to, imposes itself on anyone who has been around for even a little while.

By the same token, just as the need for inquiry announces itself, so also does its successful close. In so far as the question posed by the situation in which he finds himself is once more a familiar question to the agent, one congruous with tried ways of behaving, there is nothing more to inquire about. The tension and conflict characterizing the inclusive situation of the agent, and springing from his "being-at-a-loss" in the face of insistent requirements, have been resolved. Harmony has been restored.

This does not mean, of course, that the solution to one question may not give rise to new conflicts or that there is ever a time when man's experience as responsible agent is so harmonious, his habits so proportioned to the full range of the demands placed upon him, that there is no room for further inquiry. Indeed, one of the points I shall try to make is that the very breadth of man's "environment" precludes his ever wholly taming it. The unlimited character of *the other* involved in man's life prevents the question raised by that life from ever becoming wholly familiar. The integration and harmony, therefore, of the responding agent's experience is so far from ever being a stable possession that it is actually never more than an ideal. The measure of actual at-home-ness man achieves is never more than relative to some limited range of the other. Even this limited wholeness is possible only by a selective restriction of man's attention to his more urgent and pressing perplexities—those that must be resolved for life to continue at all, or at least without excessive disruption. But the moment he lifts his eyes beyond these, there are always others. Indeed, being perplexed is so much a part of man's awareness of himself in the world, that any integration presenting itself as more than partial, as not leaving the door open to further and continuing inquiry, is by that very fact grasped as not even partial, as being wholly and radically inadequate.

For all this, however, particular and limited inquiries are successfully concluded; particular tensions and conflicts are, as a matter of fact, resolved; relatively reliable habits are acquired which are then available for inclusion within more comprehensively satisfactory integrations. Were it not for the self-evident character of such limited successes, were it not that under specific conditions and by certain operations manifest confusion can be transformed into manifest coherence, neither inquiry nor anything like human reasonableness and intelligence could arise and develop in the first place.

Before concluding this first section on the general nature of inquiry, one final word. The insistence I have placed on responsible action as the originating ground and ultimate context of inquiry—that alone in terms of which "taking thought" itself becomes a meaningful activity—should not be misconstrued to imply the final servitude of inquiry to immediately and overtly practical ends imposed on man from without, or the one-sided and exclusive domination of thinking by practice. On the contrary, the real significance of referring inquiry to human action for its meaning is to place that action under the illumination and direction of thought, to allow man to take into account in his practice more than what is immediately at hand. As we shall see, far from being limited to simply discovering means for pre-established ends, human inquiry includes within its scope the progressive determination of the goals themselves of human endeavor.

2. *The Matrix and Scope of Philosophical Inquiry.* So far, we have considered inquiry in relation to the active life of man. The point of this section is to view it in relation to man's communal life. For the responsible self, whose experience as responder inquiry seeks to integrate, exists and functions only in a community of selves. And this, I shall maintain, has important—and too often overlooked—bearings not only on the nature of

inquiry in general, but also on the origin and nature of philosophical inquiry specifically.

Human experience is essentially *shared* experience. The environment with which man interacts is not simply and utterly
physical. It is not engaged merely in terms of its immediate
impingement on the human organism. It is dealt with primarily
as being also for others, as being something *in common*. Things
are imbued with meanings that have arisen in a context of cooperative activity which involves common and shared ways of
intending and relating to them. In fact, it is only as ingredient
in community action, that is, as dealt with in common, that
elements of the environment acquire objective status vis-à-vis the
human self and become things to which the human self can
respond and not merely react. In other words, man the responder
emerges only as sharing a way of life with other selves, only as
participating in a common culture, only as member of an ongoing community, an ongoing cooperative enterprise. It is
through the acquisition of shared habits of belief and practice,
a kind of induction into a common system of interpretations
and valuations which regulate the cooperative relation of members of the group towards the environment and one another,
that self-awareness and the capacity to act responsibly arise and
mature.

If this is the case, then it is clear that there can be no question
of any inquiry that does not presuppose, and proceed against the
background of, the more or less coherent world-view of the
group in and by which the inquirer has been formed. Before
he can even experience any kind of incoherence in his life as
responsible agent, he has already been accustomed to viewing
and relating to his surroundings in the way the community does
of which he is a member, and this cultural influence cannot but

affect the way he sees his problem and the sort of solution he will find acceptable.

Secondly, it must be remembered that the shared system of regulative meanings and procedures has a double import. Of first importance is its role, as shared, in the creation of community. This it has almost regardless of its contents, that is, regardless of what precisely is commonly believed and prized. I say "almost," because it is clear that no way of life can be viable that completely disregards, or is not in some measure adequate to, the actual conditions of human survival. Granted that there is this minimal adequacy, however, the traditions of the group, whatever they happen to be, are an essential condition for its very being and life as a human community. Precisely as shared, they are what makes and keeps the community and its members human.

However, besides their adequacy in the role of making a common life possible, there is also the matter of their adequacy to the real possibilities of man in relation to his environment, that is, of human experience as a whole. Here the question of content, of what is believed and what is prized, comes to the fore. For if the sharing of beliefs is what constitutes life human in the first place, the relative adequacy of their contents to actual conditions and possibilities determines the richness of that life, its greater or lesser humanity.

This distinction between the role of beliefs as shared and their adequacy in terms of content has significant bearings on an understanding of the nature of inquiry. First of all, it indicates why shared beliefs are already goods—and tend to be held on to —regardless of the amount of evidence that can be brought to support or undermine them. Their initial elaboration and the credence given them is more a function of the requirements of community, of the need for a comprehensive and common way of life, than it is of adequacy to the real natures of things. Quite apart from this latter question, their very serviceability in the creation and maintenance of community already gives them a kind of validity.

On the other hand, the very fact that a common way of intending the elements and make-up of human life arises with only minimal regard for their inherent possibilities is precisely what makes its subsequent criticism and correction by the responsible agent to which it gives rise not only necessary but inevitable. For the responsible agent cannot long be satisfied with the mere adaptation and application of common sense, that generally accepted body of regulative meanings and procedures, to particular circumstances. Such application does, of course, entail a kind of inquiry. In this case, however, inquiry's only function is to bridge the gap between accepted norms and particular cases. It is not a matter of radically extending or revising traditional ways but simply of providing them with that final determination which is necessary for their functioning in the *here and now*.

However, another and critical kind of inquiry, one concerned not merely with the application but with the very adequacy of common sense, cannot in the long run fail to emerge. Common sense inevitably comes under scrutiny because of its built-in disproportion to the very self-awareness it makes possible. The responsible agent, as we have seen, cannot but be aware of the general connection between what he does and what he undergoes. He knows that the satisfaction of needs and the securing of goods and enjoyments depends on the way he actively intervenes in his surroundings. The adequacy of his response is conditioned by the measure in which he has actually discriminated the factors

45

functioning within the experimental process and determined their connections with one another and with the quality of his life. In other words, the world is grasped as *means* (that is, as instrumental) to *consummatory* experience so that its intelligent use presupposes a knowledge of its workings, of what is connected with what. The greater this knowledge, the greater man's capacity for intelligent response.

Now common sense gives rise to this awareness, but cannot by itself, that is, by its own meanings and procedures, do much about it. Its absorption with the qualitative, with direct uses and enjoyments, although it involves a knowledge of objects independent of the agent, precludes a knowledge of them in their independence, that is, precisely as objects. Such a knowledge, which is a pre-requisite for the intelligent exploitation of the *world-as-means*—that is, a knowledge in which things are defined precisely in terms of their relationships to one another rather than in terms of direct experience—can arise only by setting aside immediately practical concerns and putting into play the operations and procedures of scientific inquiry. From this point of view, scientific inquiry is a necessary development and refinement of the responsible agent's interpretation of the world-as-means. It is occasioned by the discrepancy between the question posed by the world-as-means and the agent's equipment in terms of common sense to deal with it, and its function as inquiry is to resolve this discrepancy.

Common sense, however, is not only inadequate to the possibilities of the world-as-means; it is also inherently inadequate to the possibilities of human life itself as consummatory end. To emerge, through participation in a common way of life, into responsible self-awareness is to reach a point beyond that way of life, a point from which that way of life itself becomes questionable. It is to be in a position not only to judge its quality and coherence, its concrete reasonableness as an esthetic whole but, insofar as this way of life is regulative of the community's activities, to be called on to justify it. A critical justification, however, of common sense meanings and procedures cannot be carried on in terms of those meanings and procedures. For this, a new and this time philosophical inquiry is needed, one that looks to all these meanings precisely as meanings, both in their relationships to one another and to the over-all quality of life. From this point of view, philosophy will be an inquiry into the coherence, quality, "sense" of human life itself as comprehensive reality and final value. It will arise because of the discrepancy in man's experience as responder between the question posed by human life-as-end and the habitual equipment of common sense to deal with it. And once again, its function will be to resolve this discrepancy.

Philosophical inquiry, therefore, no less than other forms of inquiry, emerges in response to tensions and conflicts inherent in human life itself. No less than they, it aims at a qualitative transformation of experience. As Blondel once observed, its purpose is not so much to explain life as to constitute it, to lift it to a level of integrity and coherence that cannot be reached without it. This being so, we can understand why philosophy cannot divorce or separate itself from the ongoing course of life and the actual concerns of men if it is to be true to itself and not self-defeating. Because it bears on the quality of life itself, it must begin there and end there. Not artificial or contrived issues are its starting-point, but the actual shape of life as it is lived in the world today. Nor is its goal to reach some realm behind or beyond the affairs of everyday, but to order and integrate these same affairs into something coherent and whole.

From this, we can understand why agreement among philosophers is so difficult of attainment. If philosophy is indeed an inquiry into the possible sense and coherence of human life as end-value, any completely objective test for determining the relative validity of its results is out of the question. For the kind of coherence which life can have for a person are not independent of his desires, expectations and aspirations—that is, of his individual bias, both that which is spontaneous and that which is culturally conditioned. All of these inevitably enter into a judgment of the adequacy of a view of life purporting to be comprehensive.

It is here that philosophy is in a different position from that occupied by science. The connections prevailing in the world-as-means are independent of our likes and dislikes. Conflicting views as to what they are can be adjudicated by the sort of control they respectively make possible. The very fact that a particular interpretation makes possible a successful use of the world as means which another does not, precludes any argument about their relative merits. In philosophy, however, no such experiment is possible. In the presence of conflicting philosophies, a person will incline to that in whose light his own orientation and relationships to the surrounding universe make the most sense. As an inclusive and comprehensive quality, such "sense" is final and ultimate, with nothing outside it to certify its presence. A particular philosophy does not enable its adherent to do anything he otherwise could not do. Rather, it enables him to experience his life differently, viz. as more coherent and meaningful, than would otherwise be possible.

This difference of immediate quality—which is a matter of

direct awareness, something a person can feel and testify to but not prove—is the decisive factor in shaping philosophical convictions. A person will hold that view which, to him, affords or promises the greatest harmony and integration of life's complexity. And, let us face it, different individuals, with different backgrounds, biases and preoccupations, are always going to see things differently. This is not to say that all views are equally valid or that an immediate quality of coherence may not have resulted from an oversight of relevant factors which subsequent experience—most notably discussion with other philosophers—may force on the attention of the thinker and so require a modification of his outlook. It is only to say that the only real test of man's efforts to rationalize life's possibilities is the on-going course of life itself. On the purely intellectual level, there is no hypothesis of such universal appeal as to preclude opposition, nor any so implausible as not to win some adherents.

When speaking of integration and coherence, therefore, we have to distinguish between a kind of preliminary and provisional integration of a person's life which is achieved apart from others in personal reflection, and that ultimate integration of it which is achieved in universal communion. Only as found in the long run—which is longer than any of us will be around—to reliably promote such all-inclusive harmony can philosophic conceptions be with full warrant asserted as adequate. Short of this long run, we can only grope toward communion through dialogue and discussion in an effort to purify our separate visions and intentions of all those elements which keep them separate and discrepant.

3. *The Modes of Philosophical Inquiry.* We have defined all inquiry as man's continuing effort to integrate his experience as

responsible agent. We have distinguished philosophy from other forms of inquiry as that which looks to the comprehensive integration of this experience, the integration of human life as end. What we want to do now is briefly indicate three distinct, but interconnected, steps in this effort.

(a) *Logic.* Man as responsible agent emerges to self-awareness through participation with others in common ways of intending his environment. For any individual these common ways in the form of acquired habits are a presupposition of his capacity for self-direction. He has them before he is in any position to judge them critically. The same can be said of the community as a whole. Its common habits were not developed reflectively but in response to various and direct existential needs. They hang together as a kind of vital system, not an immediately logical one. Their critical scrutiny, however, is not something that can be put off indefinitely.

To be aware of a variety of regulative meanings whose justification to be such is not immediately evident is, for a responsible agent, to be called on to justify them. The first step in such a justification is to seek to relate them to one another as meanings. Unless they can be reflectively grasped as logically hanging together and forming a coherent whole, the agent's own life as shaped by them cannot be grasped as whole. Whatever kind of sense it may make so long as he does not think about it, it will lack the moment he does. The inherent tension of such a situation, therefore, inevitably gives rise to an effort to think through habitual meanings in order to make sense of them on the level of thought. This is a first condition for an adequate philosophy —theoretical coherence. If a philosophy falls short here, then, whatever other virtues it may possess, it is inherently inadequate to that unification of experience which is its *raison d'être.*

(b) *Phenomenology.* However, mere theoretical coherence is not enough. For it is a notorious fact that meanings intended as meanings have a kind of life of their own. They can be linked up, spun out and developed into logical patterns almost as things in themselves without regard for the context in which they arose and functioned. The result is that in the search for an interpretation of life that can be thought through consistently, sheer notional coherence can come to be emphasized at the expense of practical relevance. A philosophy can be elaborated that has nothing to do with the very life from which it arose and of which it was supposed to be an interpretation, nothing to do with human experience except as a kind of springboard for taking off into the blue.

Needless to say, instead of integrating the agent's experience, such efforts only serve to exacerbate its divisions and discords. Indeed, in place of harmony, interpretations of this kind actually introduce new and gratuitous splits which cannot but distract the inquiring mind from what it originally set out to do. Thus, for example, we find philosophies which actually dig an unbridgeable chasm between their chosen realm of the "really real," accessible only to thought, and a disparaged realm of "mere appearance" which, unfortunately is where we live. What could be more absurd and yet what, unfortunately, is more commonplace than the philosopher whose theoretical convictions are so divorced from his practice that to engage in the latter he must forget the former?

Now the point I am trying to make is that theoretical coherence is a snare and, in the end, self-defeating when it is not complemented and continually tested by what we may call phenomenological adequacy. In other words, just as the agent's experience lacks coherence so long as he cannot think his life, so also is coherence lacking when he cannot live his thought. In addition to being self-consistent, an adequate philosophic stance must also hang together with what is disclosed in direct experience, with all that the agent is and can become aware of from his life together with others in community. It is, after all, this same concrete life that he seeks to integrate.

(c) *Meta-pragmatics.* However, self-consistency and adequacy to what is already disclosed in the very living of life are not enough to constitute an adequate philosophy. If philosophical inquiry is man's effort to integrate his whole experience as responsible agent, then, since philosophy itself is one of the things he does, it must itself come under its own purview and relate itself to that aspiration for wholeness which animates it and which it in turn seeks to implement and fulfill.

In other words, philosophy must self-consciously place itself in the context and service of human life of which it is a function and whose direction it has to grasp both to control its own conduct as inquiry and to measure the adequacy of its results. This means, first of all, the formulation of an ideal of human wholeness, a determination in reflection of the sort of coherence to which man inherently aspires. Secondly, it means a work of continuous criticism carried on in the light of this ideal—a criticism not only of common-sense beliefs and practices but also of the shape and results of our philosophical efforts as well. If all human efforts are ultimately for the enhancement of human life itself as comprehensive end-value, then they all-including the philosophical—must be judged in terms of their bearing on the pervasive quality of that life, that is, in terms of the contribution they make, negative or positive, to its wholeness, coherence, concrete reasonableness, ultimate satisfactoriness. Supposing, as I do, that this ultimate coherence and satisfactoriness consists in the achievement of universal personal community, then it will be in terms of their bearing on such an achievement that all our efforts must be judged. The making of such judgments about all that man does—including, therefore, his philosophical efforts and their issue—is, I submit, the primary and abiding task of philosophical inquiry.

When this is remembered and acted on, then not only is philosophy saved from the kind of irrelevance into which it has too often fallen, but it becomes the most powerful instrument at life's disposal for life's own rational reconstruction and final achievement.

PART TWO

SITUATION

Ideas have consequences; they are plans for action. Any mistake in the plans is inevitably an obstacle to growth. What a man believes—about himself, about the world, about God—will control the way he develops, the richness (or poverty) of his life.

The important thing is to keep all the avenues open, to see things not merely in their differences but in their connections and relationships, their capacity to complement and reinforce one another. For nothing is sealed off from anything else. Man is continuous with nature, spirit with matter, the individual with the community, the divine with the human. The continuities are more fundamental than the distinctions.

Life advances by means of encounters and syntheses. Its meanings are the issue of genuine interactions. The secret is to see the other not as enemy but as ally—one's co-agent in the promotion of a richer reality where each thing, in union with the rest, is more fully itself. The final reality is personal communion.

III.

Matter and Spirit

ONE of the difficulties with a spiritualist anthropology is its tendency to make man a stranger in the world. For some thinkers, to hold that man is spirit, albeit *embodied spirit,* is to hold that he has access to another world besides this one, another world that is his true home. As spiritual, man may be *in* the world but is really not *of* it. He is only "passing through."

The commonest form of this error is what might be called the "two lives" theory. Man is thought to have two lives side by side, corresponding to the two components of his nature. He has an outer, *bodily* life of interaction with the world, and an inner, *spiritual* life that lifts him above the world. The outer life is concerned with time, the inner life with eternity. The outer life is confused, full of contradictions, loose ends and leftovers. The inner life is one of light and peace; it is serenely whole.

If an effort is made to interrelate these two lives, the connection envisaged is usually one of subordination. The outer life is for the inner life. Man must attend to his biological needs, fill his stomach, have energy to think. Moreover, since his is a spirit of the lowest order, with no innate resources, it requires nourishment from the senses to have something to think about. Man's bodily life is thus a kind of springboard for his spirit. He needs

57

it, but only to get off the ground. And "off the ground," beyond space and time, is where he belongs.

At first glance, this doctrine may seem ennobling. By concentrating on the inner life, it sets man's sights on the timeless and enduring instead of on the fleeting and insubstantial. Moreover, what better motive for keeping our bodily lusts in check, for not giving our hearts to the things around us or becoming too wrapped up with them, than the assurance that "we have not here a lasting city," that the only importance of bodily life is to make our spiritual life possible?

Yet, despite its apparent warrant, the "two-lives" theory could hardly be more mistaken or mischievous. By making man an angel incarnate, it not only dehumanizes him but brutalizes the world. As Dewey once remarked, to pursue the spiritual in isolation from matter is to play into the hands of the crudest kind of materialism, to become a "conspirator with the sensual mind." For the materialist is not one who cares too much about his bodily life. Rather he is one who does not care enough. He lives on the surface of things, seeking only to extract a kind of private enjoyment from them and unconcerned about the genuine possibilities his life in the world opens up to him.

And this is the point. Human spirituality does not mean access to another world, but a *new intimacy* with this one. It releases a whole new range of possible relationships that are completely beyond the capacities of the merely material.

The merely material is, to be sure, involved in interaction with its surroundings. But the interaction is blind, and either locked in routine or wildly random. Moreover, its closest connections to its neighbors are purely functional. Alongside others and even sustained by them, it is never *near* them, never *with* them. What is only material is closed in on itself, objectively unaware, plunged in solitude.

With man, all this is changed. The givenness of matter still conditions his life but no longer defines it. Situated in a world of others he is not shut off from them. Unlike the merely material, his very being is a *being with*. In place of routine and randomness, it is intelligence that characterizes human relationships—intelligence, and choice, and responsiveness, and the sheer joy of a joint effort. Brute matter is indifferent and unconcerned; man, as also spiritual, can appreciate and nurture and care.

Instead of alienation, therefore, spirituality spells deeper involvement. It flowers, not in withdrawal, but in *nearness,* in love. For the endless Beyond that calls to spirit is really a "Beyond in our midst." It is the Depth of things and their Ground, and only as such can we reach it. In our effort to respond to the infinite import of each of our acts, we embrace God Himself along with our world. *Here,* in the *human deed,* is where He dwells.

Thus man has not two lives, but one. Neither a part-time body nor a spirit on the side, man is called to be wholly and integrally human. For in this human, worldly life, everything is involved, including God. Only in the measure we enter into it can we know fulfillment.

Being, Power and Conflict

One of the promising feaures of contemporary thought is its new awareness of the personal. One of its dangers, however, is that this awareness easily degenerates into sentimentalism.

The distinctive value of the person is too often emphasized at the expense of his continuity with the rest of nature. This results in thinking of the person as somehow exempted by right from the pain, conflict and struggle that characterize the whole evolutionary process. Whereas, in the rest of nature, creative advance is inevitably tied up with tension and opposition, the person is apparently entitled to "fulfillment without bother." Because he has the right never to be used as a mere thing, he has also—so it is thought—the right never to be resisted or opposed. Force is felt to be incompatible with his dignity. Simply as a person, he claims approval, no matter how he behaves.

Such woolly minded escapism is actually a rejection of finitude. It forgets that tensions, conflicts and the continuous testing of strength are not the hallmark of brute, impersonal nature but of finite being itself. Men are locked in struggle, not because they have somehow failed, but simply because they are men. As Tillich observes: "Every encounter, whether friendly or hostile, whether benevolent or indifferent, is in some way, unconsciously or consciously, a struggle of power with power." To be scandalized by this is to be scandalized by the real. To ignore it is to court disaster.

The inevitability of conflict between persons rests on the fact that being means power and power implies otherness and opposition. To be at all is to be powerful, to have the capacity to meet resistance successfully, to be able to stand up to otherness. In the absence of resistance, not only does a given amount of power remain untested and undefined; it is completely lacking in meaning. This is true of the least particle of matter. And it is true, no less, of the person. Up and down the scale of being, the thrust of each thing is to come to the best possible terms with its surroundings, that is, terms proportionate to the actual powers involved.

That there are different levels of power goes without saying. If each thing is called to face up to otherness by means of its own resources, it does so in a way correlative to those resources. The purely material, for example, is essentially involved as an element in a larger process. Its task is to carve out a space for itself by neutralizing opposing forces and achieving a kind of balance. The power of life extends farther. A living thing is not merely involved in process but is itself a process. It seeks not merely space, but growth; not merely to neutralize the other, but to draw nourishment from it. The power of the person, however, is the highest of all. Its confrontation with otherness involves more than the effort to maintain physical integrity in the face of invading forces, more too than the struggle to eke out a living by converting the other into itself. The proper task of the person, and the one proportionate to his power, is to incorporate in his life the other precisely as other. It is to make of his life a comprehensive synthesis, interior to which both self and other are preserved in their distinctiveness. This is what is meant by saying that the person is called to community. It also provides the basic problem of personal life.

The problem of community, which is the form of personal life, is the one of deciding on whose terms it shall be lived. Simply to impose my terms on the other person is to deny his freedom and responsibility; simply to accept his terms without demur is to abandon my own. In either case, there is no community but a kind of fusion or absorption instead. For community implies a mutuality of distinct initiatives that can never exist as something settled once and for all, but only as an ongoing project. This is why the order of persons is an order of continuous and inevitable tension. Without the continuous struggle to come to terms acceptable to both parties and compromising the reality of neither, a truly personal union cannot be achieved. But struggle implies power. One does not enter the lists armed only with good will and kind thoughts. Besides a readiness to search out what is objectively fair, one needs the force also to resist what falls short of it.

Love without power is not enough, because love without power soon ceases to be love. Without the strength to resist encroachments, openness to the other comes down simply to "giving in." The person, then, is called to do battle; there is no advance without it. If he is also called to know peace, it is because peace is not a state but a process, not just a matter of avoiding conflicts but of keeping our conflicts constructive.

Permanence and Change

We are living in an age when the past is coming unstuck. Traditional values and patterns are no longer operative. The popular press is filled with articles about our changing morality, and General Eisenhower is not alone in taking a decidedly dim view of the way things are going.

But despite the gravity of our present situation, it has its brighter side. For, as Max Scheler once observed, if traditional patterns make possible a certain kind of progress, human development also demands a gradual loosening of their hold. The purpose, then, of the following remarks is to indicate how our present predicament is also an opportunity.

The importance of traditional patterns, quite apart from their content, is based on the role of habit in human life. More than a child of reason, man is a creature of habits and needs them in order to act. For habits represent that large-scale adjustment to his surroundings, which is presupposed for his pursuit of particular goals and the satisfaction of his immediate needs. Only by being able to take the over-all framework of his activity for granted is his mind freed to work out the details and concerns of everyday life. To have to attend to everything at once would bring that life to a standstill.

This is the reason why periods of change like the present are so unsettling. The collapse of habitual frameworks calls everything we do in question. The very foundations of our familiar world are brushed aside and replaced with problems. Small wonder, when change goes so deep, if it seems to be for the worse.

But there is another side to all this, which is the point of Scheler's remark. For the fact that certain modes of adjustment become habitual is not without its own dangers. The price for freedom of attention at short range can be a kind of mental paralysis at longe range. By subtracting our practical framework and general mode of behavior from the area of direct attention, habit obscures the fact that these are not the only ones possible and that they can always be improved. We become set in our ways. What began as adjustment winds up as rigidity. Indeed, because they have become the unconscious presupposition of our everyday existence, the workings of habit are sometimes confused with principle, and a relative, temporal pattern becomes a timeless norm.

There is, to be sure, something timeless in man. If there were not, he would not be aware of time. Only by having a foothold outside the rush of change can he know it is taking place. But however much this timeless element is pressed into the mold of our habits, it never becomes one with them. In fact, far from endorsing their fixity, it is a motive for breaking their grip.

For the timeless in man is not any settled pattern of determination. Patterns arise in process and disappear the same way. The timeless in man is his selfhood, that point where he hears God's voice. It is his awareness of other persons and his permanent vocation to promote their welfare. It is his freedom to change his mind, to regret his past and mend his ways. The timeless in man is his openness to the Infinite, which prevents anything yet accomplished from being the final word. With the Absolute for his horizon, his future dwarfs his past, and what he has achieved is as nothing compared with what is still to be done.

Here we have the brighter side of our present state. The contemporary breakdown of habits forces man to reassess his ways, to recognize the limitations inherent in current procedures. He is called upon once more to situate his large-scale behavior in the context of the Eternal and try to make it less inadequate to the full range of his possibilities. By compelling him to take a stand on issues he would otherwise have neglected, the collapse of habit makes possible a wider, richer achievement. In short, only the discomfort of crisis keeps habit from becoming a rut and the eternal in man from going completely to sleep.

Creativity

Man today is struggling painfully toward a new conception of himself, a new ideal. Some of the implications of this ideal were outlined by the late Dr. Richard Niebuhr in his book *The Responsible Self*. Our young people, however, are the ones who have really felt its appeal and are dramatically mobilizing their energies around it.

The central components of the new ideal are "responsibility" and "creativity." The notion of responsibility, to which Dr. Niebuhr directed his attention, suggests the "image of man-the-answerer, man engaged in dialogue, man acting in response to action upon him." Man's life is viewed as a process of interaction with the natural, social and religious forces that make up his environment, and its meaning hangs on the sort of response he gives to them.

What this response should be is suggested by the second component: creativity. The image of creativity is drawn from the fine arts. Man is an artist called to shape the stuff of daily experience into something more adequately expressive both of his own originality as a person and of that transcendent plenitude to which, as a person, he is open. His encounter with his surroundings is meant to be a creative process in which both they and he are fulfilled. This means that the world of man is essentially open to change. It is there to be transformed, not merely endured. Like the artist struggling with a stubborn medium, whose possibilities he can only gradually realize and never exhaust, man is called continually to grapple with the world around him with a view to its endless enhancement.

To set up "creative responsibility" as an ideal has important consequences. For one thing, action becomes primary. The meaning of a man's life is the difference his presence makes in the over-all process. To go through the world unconcerned about its state is to miss out completely. Being human means coming to grips creatively with the concrete situation in which a person finds himself.

Secondly, thought is viewed as basically practical. Its overriding aim is to find out what is going on. For if man is to respond and not just react, improve matters and not just complicate them, he must have as accurate a grasp as possible of what he is dealing with. The role of thought is to provide this interpretative grasp.

Such concentration on the here and now, it should be noted, does not rule out philosophy. The over-all sense of a situation is not irrelevant to my practical decisions. But the philosophy in question must seek to provide this sense. Its conceptual schemes must come to grips with process and history, be open to novelty, leave room for surprises. As with all thought, its function is to understand how things are, not dictate how they must be.

Thirdly, this new ideal puts a premium on personal freedom. If creative responsibility means anything, it means determining before God the appropriate response to a situation and acting accordingly. This, of course, does not exempt an individual from submission to human authority. Authoritative structures, deserving obedience, are part and parcel of man's world. But they can never be final or absolute. Not only must they continually recommend themselves by their reasonableness to the persons they are meant to serve, but, like all other human devices, they too stand in need of constant criticism and constant improvement.

One more point. Creative responsibility is non-ideological in the sense of non-utopian. It does not aim at any final state of affairs, but simply at the next step. Just as the past is important only as something accomplished and now to be surpassed, so there can be no future that will not also call for new exertions. The one thing for a man to do is to tackle whatever he finds at hand and leave it in some way better than he found it.

Needless to say, administrators of today's institutions are not generally the most ardent advocates of this new stance. Its inherent discontent with the status quo puts them under constant fire. Moreover, the vagueness of its objectives and its seeming cult of novelty for its own sake make it appear a threat to right order. But the threat, I suggest, is more apparent than real. For there is an order here—it is man's ordination to Being, his abiding vocation as Being's agent. And there is a touchstone, too, for distinguishing better from worse—the touchstone of intelligent recognition. If openness to Being is truly constitutive of man, then we all share a common light by which to judge whether any steps proposed are really improvements, or not. But even more profoundly, we all share a common calling to move beyond where we are if we are going to be true to ourselves.

In short, creative responsibility is devotion to Being itself. It is service of the Infinite in and through the finite, man's part in God's own work of promoting and expanding His presence among men. Its root is the Love that made the world and is ever restless to better it.

Responsibility for the Future

Central to the thought of Teilhard de Chardin is that man is the spearhead of evolution. In and through man, world process becomes conscious and self-directing. This means that the future is now up to us. God looks to us to complete His work. He makes the outcome of creation dependent on our free response. Although He made us without us, Augustine declares, He cannot save us without us.

The obscure realization of this awful responsibility is the root of that nameless and haunting anxiety which is part of being human. All the entities beneath man run their course more or less automatically. They do what they do because they are what they are. But man, however much he too is involved in the determinisms of nature, nevertheless in his personal core stands apart from nature and above it. The very fact that he is conscious of himself and can step back from his environment to survey it, puts within his hands the power to shape history.

With man's emergence from nature, the world becomes unstuck. What happens now is no longer the simple result of what has gone before. The future—even the question as to whether or not there will be one—is henceforth a matter of decision. As Scheler has pointed out, to be man is in a sense to stand on the brink of nothingness. It is to stare into the void and know that God Himself cannot sustain us unless we decide to let Him.

Small wonder if clear and abiding awareness of the role he is called to play is almost too much for man to stand. Small wonder, too, if he experiences his freedom less as a precious privilege than as a burden he can hardly support. Hence it is that, having slipped the bonds of nature and its inexorable routines, man immediately sets about devising new routines of his own—routines in which he can newly lose himself, can be swept along without thinking and be freed from the need to decide. From that perilous brink where nothing is guaranteed, he retreats to a contrived world where everything has its place in the humdrum of everyday. Even his relation to God, that partnership in innovation which should be a continual challenge to spend himself in creative effort, succumbs to a deadening routinism. Religion itself is made a comfortable matter of regular, weekly observance.

All this, I say, is understandable. It is even to some extent necessary. Man's limited powers of attention make routine and habit indispensable parts of his action. Wholesale anxiety and questioning, at least when not tempered by hope, would freeze him in his tracks. Moreover, it might be argued that to set up routines and patterns, which introduce order and regularity into an otherwise chaotic world, is precisely the contribution that man is called on to make. The institution of routines could then be seen as the triumph of reason and control over irrational caprice. Perhaps. But the triumph is limited and precarious. And this we must not lose sight of.

For routines have a way of swallowing the whole of life and deadening all sense of crisis. Their mere existence is taken as their own guarantee and as an excuse for the individual to concern himself, not with the fate of the world, but with the pursuit of his private interests. The fact that they imitate nature makes our routines seem part of the given. We forget that whatever order exists in human affairs has been painfully achieved and that its maintenance and promotion remains our individual responsibility. However much we may think otherwise, our future cannot be assured without our efforts. It is guaranteed only in the measure that we singly and collectively work at it.

In November 1963 the world was shaken by tragedy. The following month we celebrated Christmas. The two facts are not unrelated. President Kennedy's death revealed to us all how fragile and vulnerable the devices of man really are, how little they can be relied on to take care of themselves, how narrowly they separate us from the brink of nothingness that defines our condition. Christmas, on the other hand, reminds us that we still have a future to strive for. Despite our past failures, God continues to come to us and seeks with our co-operation to set up the reign of His peace. Perhaps we are beginning to realize how the world hangs on the response which we, each of us, give Him.

The Dimensions of Time

It is often said that modern man has discovered time. This, I think, is only half true. For, what he has discovered is but one of time's dimensions. The other, which he still overlooks, is really the one that can save him.

The dimension of time which science has disclosed is its horizontal sweep and it would be hard to overestimate the revolution it has wrought in man's conception of himself and of the world. As R. G. Collingwood pointed out in his little classic, *The Idea of Nature,* how the world looks to us depends very much on how long we take to observe it. "If, for example, an historian had no means of apprehending events that occupied more than an hour, he could describe the burning down of a house but not the building of a house; the assassination of Caesar but not his conquest of Gaul; the performance of a symphony but not its composition." And, he goes on to say, since making things normally takes longer than destroying them, the shorter our temporal perspective for viewing historical events, the more our history will consist of destruction, catastrophes, battle, murder and sudden death.

The point is clear. Prior to the techniques of modern science and the discoveries of paleontology, man was inevitably myopic. He had absolutely no way of conceiving the enormously long, slow process by which his familiar world had laboriously built itself up. Hence his radical suspicion of change. Unable to imagine how the existing order could gradually come into being, he necessarily viewed it as something divinely established and given from the beginning—something that could only be changed for the worse. For him, contemporary developments were always a decline from the good old days of the golden past.

With modern man, the picture is reversed. *Process, change* and *development* are the very passwords to truth. In the light of evolution, order is not a presupposition but an accomplishment. There is nothing that exists today of any significant complexity that has not emerged from a simpler past. Instead of being behind him, therefore, the golden age lies ahead. Mankind is not declining; it is barely out of its infancy. Even the paroxysms of contemporary civilization should not be viewed as a malady. They are little more than growing pains.

At first glance, all this is exciting. In contrast to the stuffy fixity of previous conceptions, this one is wide open to novelty. For repetition, it substitutes creativity; for well-defined limits, the continuous challenge to venture forth.

But, together with the excitement, there is also a strange kind of emptiness. Or better, the excitement itself somehow remains abstract. For if, in terms of this modern view, mankind has at last discovered the future, the individual seems to have lost it and lost the present as well. How, after all, can I, as an individual, existing for less than a moment in the long sweep of evolutionary process, attach any real significance to what I do? How can I take seriously my little works and pomps, or even the larger causes to which I may devote my energies? If everything is in transition, are not all my efforts doomed to be swept aside in the creative advance of Life? And if all of today's conflicts are merely the dialectical gropings of a single Life-Force, straining toward the future and syntheses not yet dreamt of, how can it make any difference where I, a bare and fleeting particle of that Force, boldly take my stand?

This is the difficulty with contemporary man's insistence on the sweep of time while ignoring its depth. The view may exalt mankind but it takes the heart out of men.

But time is not made up of a single, horizontal axis. It has a vertical one as well. This is the one that cuts right through the present moment and, whatever that moment's relative significance in the over-all march of events, endows it with infinite, eternal meaning. For the present is not mere transition. The *now* is not just an infinitesimal dot on the endless line of becoming. The *now* is also that moment where I stand before the Lord and say Yes or No to Him. However slight the mark of my deeds on the course of history, they each bear the absolute weight of acceptance or rejection of God. If they are deeds of love, so that He has a part in them, then this makes up their true substance—a substance which cannot fade—no matter how fleeting their shape.

This is the saving force of the present. Man has indeed been called by God to build a world, a vocation whose import he has perhaps only lately begun to realize. But because it is God who calls him, he need not wait forever for fulfillment. No less than for his grandparents, the crucial time for modern man is, as it always was, now.

IV.

The Power of Love

MUCH has been written about love. But most of the writing, as Père Teilhard de Chardin has remarked, concerns "only the sentimental face of love, the joy and miseries it causes us." Relatively little has been set down about love as a way of life. And the power of love, which is the power of Being itself, has been all but passed over.

Some inkling of love's power can be had by each of us if we but recall those rare and privileged moments when, with sudden splendor, the brightness of love burst into our lives.

There we were, wrapped up with ourselves and lost in a seemingly indifferent world. We had allowed ourselves to become harassed by care and anxiety, absorbed with our immediate preoccupations, oppressed by the bleak business of coping with every day. Then suddenly the veil lifted. Through a chance encounter, an unexpected kindness, the sheer radiance of a loving glance, all the more precious because unhoped for and unmerited, Being beckoned to us. However momentarily, we caught a glimpse of the world beyond care. We came alive. Possibilities for existing in ways we had forgotten, in ways that made our past routines appear a barren desert—possibilities that summoned forth a creativity we did not know we had, that infinitely enriched our present by holding up to us a future without bounds

—newly quickened our minds and hearts. Even a moment in love's presence awakened us to life and we knew the truth in Wilhelmsen's beautiful phase: "What being-*loved* makes being do is precisely *be*."

Of course, the moment was quickly gone; the humdrum resumed its sway. But we make an abiding mistake if we assume that, because the exaltation did not last—indeed, in a world frayed by time, could not last—we did not really see anything, that it was all illusion. Love's moment, even if only remembered, has a message for us. It speaks to us about ourselves and discloses within us a capacity and power that, but for love's revelation, we might never have come to know.

The reason why an encounter with love moves us so deeply is that, no matter how humble and fleeting the gesture that embodies it, it dramatically recalls to us our own vocation as persons. For the person is not a mere element caught up in nature's restless process. His role and significance cannot be measured simply in terms of specific endowments and needs or the relative place he occupies in some larger scheme. In the person, the transcendent power and creative freedom of God Himself are unleashed in their own right. To be a person is to share in Being itself and in Being's creative concern for all that is. It is to have and exercise Being's power to cherish something for its own sake, regardless of return. The person who lives as a person is the one in whom that pure devotion-to-being which *is* Being has gained untrammeled sway and shines forth in every deed. He is the one who has learned that to be is to love, to spend oneself for others that they may more truly be, and that in the spending one is not impoverished but ever more deeply rooted in that limitless abundance on which one draws.

This is the secret of love's power over us. To be loved is to encounter Being itself, eternity in time, God's face among the faces of men. The loving person translates for our benefit the exuberant life of God in human terms. He gives us a glimpse of that boundless benevolence that has sustained us from the beginning despite our heedlessness, and that seeks this very moment to erupt in our lives and organize them anew in its own image. In the one who loves us, we hear God's voice in the realm of everyday, are newly reminded of His abiding call that defines our existence as persons and with exquisite patience awaits our free response. The only thing is not to let it go unanswered.

For the vision, I have suggested, is brief. The gracious presence is abruptly withdrawn, soon consumed by death or distance, swept away by the rush of events. What was disclosed is once more concealed. Being itself, having relied on this encounter to solicit our love, quickly recedes behind the manifold determinations of everyday. And then it is only too easy to think we saw nothing at all.

The power of love, therefore, although it is the power of Being itself, is not overpowering. It intermittently stirs us, rouses us, awakens us—but it respects our freedom. Blessed is the man who recognizes it when it visits him and lets it transform his life. For only he can know what it means *to be*.

Person and Nature

The task for philosophy today is to understand, more than it has up to now, what it means to be a person. For the personal dimension has come to the fore in contemporary culture, and failure to grasp its significance underlies much of the confusion that presently besets us.

Man, to be sure, has always been personal. But in the past his personhood was interpreted largely in terms of his nature. Being a person meant the same as being a man. Who an individual was and what he was supposed to do were defined by the place he occupied in objective human society. If it was recognized that individual man somehow transcended mankind and was of absolute worth in himself, still this worth could not be realized in any other way than by sheer submission and conformity to the determinate patterns of collective human living. It was by freely assuming his place in the larger whole of concrete humanity that the individual's life made sense.

Today, however, this solution no longer seems quite adequate. For one thing, the prodigious increase in communications confronts the individual in his formative years with such a range of competing world views and traditions that automatic acceptance of any one of them is no longer possible. Right from the start, the individual experiences the need to decide for himself the meaning and scope of his life. Moreover, this heightened sense of self is further exacerbated by man's growing awareness of time and history and his increased acceptance of the idea that all determinate patterns and structures, his own human nature included, are contingent products of evolutionary development. What was once taken as fixed by eternal decree and thus able to afford the individual a stable framework is now seen as radically involved in process—a process, moreover, in which man himself is increasingly to have a hand. The individual, therefore, is no longer responsible merely for his own conforming to pre-existing patterns. He must now assume responsibility for the very patterns themselves and the shape they are henceforth to have. But a judge and shaper of patterns cannot have his meaning simply in terms of them.

This emergence of the person as an original value transcending the whole order of the factual and determinate is the chief source of man's present anxiety. He cannot simply conform to the given without abandoning his creative responsibility as a person. On the other hand, he cannot simply assert himself— which, unfortunately, is the course he is presently tempted to take—without ending up in barren isolation. As Paul Tillich has observed, the affirmation of self as part of the world and nature leads to a loss of the self, while the affirmation of self as a separate individual leads to a loss of the world. In either case, the person, who is not his own ground and can be himself only by relating to what transcends him, meets with frustration.

There is no escape from this dilemma except by seeing that beyond nature and the determinate there is, not nothing, but Being itself. Beyond the patterns, there is the patternless by excess. If the person is more than a kind of a thing, it is because his proper dynamism is that of Being itself. If he is more than a part of nature, it is because he consciously shares in nature's own ground. The Infinite, the Absolute and the Eternal all enter his very definition. The Infinite is his horizon, the Absolute his norm and the Eternal that endless moment through which all his moments pass. In short, to be a person is to be seized by Being itself as its own advocate and spokesman, indeed as its very promoter, in a world of fact and limit where it seeks always a fuller presence.

This is the reason why the person, once he has found his center, can never rest content with anything history has achieved. His aim is always a greater justice, a deeper truth, a richer love. It is also the reason why, seeking to surpass the past, he lives in profoundest continuity with it. For the person is not a mere rebel. He does not wish to break with what has been accomplished, but rather to broaden its scope. He does not seek so much to change things as to renew them. For he is Being's agent, ever reshaping the face of the earth in the light, not of his whims, but of those wider possibilities that his very presence to Being continually opens up to him.

Not the world, therefore, or nature, but Being itself, provides the wholeness within which the person is whole. In promoting the Ground of all, he heeds and enhances at the same time what is most original in himself. This is the truth that the saints have seen but that applies to each one of us. To give oneself in the service of God is to receive more than one gives. In serving the One who made him, it is the person himself who reigns.

Pain and the Human Condition

One of the hardest facts for thought to digest is the pervasive presence of pain. Yet nothing, perhaps, is more revealing about our vocation as persons.

Pain lurks everywhere. There is no action that does not cost— no worth-while action that does not cost dearly. To move is to meet with obstacles; to be conscious is to know our ignorance and limitations. Negativity is built into our very being. We need *the other* in order to exist—yet otherness means opposition and conflict. Every choice involves more than we bargain for, and what we do not choose at all we still must face. The stupid mishaps that mangle a future with a single stroke, the rejections and betrayals, the forced absences, the raw violence of sickness and death—can one wonder that our minds reel or frantically seek distraction?

Reason looks for order, a rational structure, the smooth functioning of law. The kinds of harmony it finds when it mentally isolates segments of reality for separate consideration are projected in thought to encompass the universe. Because there are relatively stable patterns within the real, reality itself must be patterned and stable. Or so we are prone to think until suffering disabuses us.

For suffering evidences the absence of a comprehensive pattern, the inadequacy of logic for coping with life. Suffering is conflict, contradiction, defeat. It is the denial from beyond ourselves of the strivings of our individual natures, the frustration from without of our natural longings. In place of a single, encompassing law reigning supreme, what we find is a clash of different laws. Instead of an over-all structure in which everything has its place, what we witness is an endless contest of opposing forces from which no one escapes unscathed.

This is the harsh fact behind much of existentialism. Human existence is too random and haphazard to be finally meaningful. So why not face it?

Up to a point, of course, the existentialist is right. Life *is* a "muddle," as William James remarked—"a muddle and a struggle." It cannot be understood in terms of a rational system, all of whose parts are functionally interrelated and all of whose states predictable in terms of what has gone before. It has the character, rather, of an ongoing drama, still unfinished and full of surprises—many of them unhappy. But to say it is therefore meaningless is a long step to take. The trouble with the existentialist is that, despite his protests to the contrary, he is still a rationalist at heart. For he accepts the rationalist premise that only the systematic is meaningful; that what is not pure geometry is pure chaos.

Actually, a look at the situation that disheartens the existentialist reveals something more than he seems to see. For if to be aware of suffering is to be called on to meet it, to take a personal stand in its presence, then neither suffering itself nor the nature it frustrates are ultimates. The mere fact of suffering still leaves open the all-important question of how we face it. If the pervasiveness of pain shows up the cracks in the world of nature and the futility of looking there for life's final meaning, the capacity of man to accept pain, to meet it nobly instead of ignobly, with courage instead of cowardice, immediately lifts him beyond the realm where it occurs.

This is the crucial point. Besides the realm of nature, this complex and haphazard process of interacting powers, there is the realm of Being itself—the Infinite in which nature participates. Indeed, it is the immanence of this "Beyond" in the realm of nature that is the root of nature's instability. Nature is, as it were, unstable by excess. It is because Being itself seeks an ever fuller presence within nature's determinate structures that none of these can ever be airtight or all-encompassing; that, in James's words, "novelty and possibility [are] forever leaking in."

Moreover, it is precisely this realm of the Absolute that constitutes man's true horizon. The context that measures man's meaning *as person* is not the finite order of conflicting determinations. Open to Being itself, man can see the relativity of the whole natural world. In the light of Being, he is able to discern what course, in the inevitable conflicts that arise, most promotes the one Value on which everything depends. This is his greatness and this is his vocation. Man is not merely an individual

81

nature looking for its own fulfillment; he is a person summoned by Love. He is called not to comfort but to creativity; not to satisfaction but to service. The price of such service runs high; it involves even death. But the stakes are higher still—they involve God Himself.

Beyond our joys and griefs, therefore, what God wants is our hearts, our utter devotion and love. In the light of this love, if we truly live it, suffering itself is transfigured.

Person and Community

One of the exciting developments of contemporary thought is its new insistence on the social character of man. That man is social by nature has long been recognized. That this trait, however, is not just one of many but is absolutely central and constitutive of man's being as person is an insight reserved to our day.

What this means is that human nature is not the possession of an individual taken by himself. Mankind is not just a collection of separate units that come together in various accidental groupings in order to satisfy their common needs. Man is essentially a community, "a community of persons in relation" (John Macmurray), and he exists only insofar as genuine community is not a dream but a reality.

To be a man, therefore, is to be a person. But to be a person is to exist only as an appeal and a response to other persons. Without the other, an other who takes account of me and for whom my free response means something, I do not exist. I can be myself only in your presence. But if I need you in order to be myself, you likewise need me. Each of us holds his "personhood" as a gift from the other, so that to betray the other is always to betray oneself. As persons, we are each of us responsible to and for the other, and only in the mutual fulfillment of this responsibility do we secure for ourselves a place in the real.

To define man as a community of persons is thus not to define what is matter of fact, something that exists in a settled and determinate way independently of the intentions of those who share in it. The reality of man is not a matter of fact but a matter of freedom. Mankind exists only as a conspiracy of individual liberties, each continually turning itself toward the others and spending itself to provide the environment in which they can flourish. For love alone is the soil in which persons grow, which furnishes the "root-room" they need to be themselves and come to full stature. But, as every lover knows, love is never a finished fact; it is always a continuing task.

To be a man, therefore, is to be essentially involved in the work of forging a world that is always new, the world of communion. This is the world which alone provides a home for man, where he can be himself and yet not alone. Only communion at once preserves the miracle of originality that is the person, while at the same time healing the isolation that became his lot when self-consciousness first wrenched him from the mothering embrace of nature. But if genuine communion is to be achieved, it must be the aim of all man's activities. It cannot play second fiddle to any of his other pursuits—to the philosophies he formulates, or the institutions he devises, or the cultures he builds. All these are devices whose ultimate meaning is to mediate the communion of persons, and they fail of their purpose when they become ends in themselves and are allowed to stand in love's way.

The task of man is thus man himself. It is unfinished business for which God has provided, as it were, only the raw materials. Mankind is thus a reality summoned to share in its own making. Since the goal of this making is a geniune community to which each member freely gives himself and, in the very giving, finds himself, responsibility for its coming to being rests with every one of us. Each person has the vocation to be for every other the vehicle of a truly creative love—indeed, of the Creator's love, in and by which alone we all live and move and are.

Authority and Fellowship

If the debate in religious circles about the conflicting claims of freedom and authority has not always been fruitful, the reason lies, I think, in the limited and univocal concept of authority too often adopted by both sides. It has been assumed without question that authority can be defined in abstraction from the sort of community in which it operates. Thus, for example, a recent essay on the use of authority in the Church quotes a definition of authority that is supposed, apparently, to apply universally and regardless of context. Authority is simply "the power in charge of unifying common actions through rules binding for all" (Yves Simon). This is inadequate.

Authority and community do, of course, go together. Community is something intentional. Persons form a community only in the measure they freely respond to a unifying intention, that is, to an act intending each of them, not in isolation, but as related to the others. This actual intention of unity, institutionally embodied and acknowledged by the plurality of persons as having a claim on them, is the power that forms community. Such power, in general, is authority.

But a community of persons can be conceived in radically different ways that profoundly affect both the role of authority and the type of response it calls for. For example, community may be conceived either as an end in itself or as a means to something else. In the latter case, we have what may be called *organic* community. This, I think, is the kind of community correlative to Simon's notion of authority. It is not formally a unity of persons, but of actions or functions. It arises from a coordination of all the various functions performed by members of the group to achieve some further good that each one has an interest in but that can be attained only by their concerted efforts. In such community, persons are not united as persons but as workers or functionaries.

In contrast to this, we have *personal* community, where the unity of persons is viewed as an end in itself. Here persons are united, not in terms of their functional relationships to a further goal, but in terms of their reality as persons. The ultimate good they seek is their loving interrelation as persons, the good of communion and fellowship. To this end, everything else is subordinated. Whatever functional relations are *also* required—to insure the ongoing life of the fellowship and make possible a common work (N.B., the work here will not be the *raison d'être* of unity but an overflow toward others of the love uniting the members)—these relations will be governed in their workings by the exigencies of communion. Thus, while organic community aims at the maximum functional efficiency consistent with the

85

fact that its functionaries are also persons, personal community aims at maximum personal reciprocity and diversifies itself in functions only as needed for such reciprocity.

In communities so different, the formulative power of community (authority) is also bound to be different. In one case, authority is indeed the power in charge of unifying actions through rules. In the other, however, it is the power dedicated to unifying persons through love. Instead of seeking primarily to impose order, authority in personal community looks to promote consensus—a genuine thinking, feeling and willing together of all the members. Whereas, in organic community, the main task of authority is to control and direct the common enterprise through binding decisions, here it is, first of all, to embody and show forth a love that encompasses all the members, and secondly, to offer itself wholeheartedly in the service of their union as a continuing catalyst of concord, a kind of focusing agent for the converging desires of the individual members to be each one for all the others as fruitfully and inclusively as possible.

Moreover, just as authority differs in the two communities, so also does the response it calls for. Since persons are involved in organic community only in terms of an aspect of themselves, namely, their function as workers, their commitment to such community and its head can never be absolute or total. It is quite properly limited to what the achievement of the goal requires. On the other hand, the universal love that animates personal community calls for a total response in kind. Any self-seeking is incompatible with the intention to be wholly for others.

This last needs emphasis today. If, in the light of our distinction, religious authorities are inconsistent when they operate "organically" and still expect total obedience, religious subjects are no less so when they think partial commitment suffices for personal community. In short, the current demand for less legalism and more love cannot be taken one-sidedly. It cuts both ways.

God and the Self

In the Preface to his play *A Man for All Seasons,* Robert Bolt writes that Thomas More "became for me a man with an adamantine sense of his own self." It is no less true, I think, that More demonstrated an adamantine sense of God and of His demands. That these two go together, that religious awareness is the correlative ground of genuine self-awareness, is the point of what follows.

One of the hazards of maintaining that God can be known by rational argument is the tendency to overlook our more immediate awareness of Him in direct experience. This is at least paradoxical. For if the word "God" does not name something already familiar in terms of our direct dealings, it is difficult to see what meaning it can have in the derivative realm of reflection.

To say, however, that God belongs to our direct experience is not without its own ambiguities. Chief among these is the meaning to be assigned "experience" in such a statement. In this connection, one thing is clear. "Experience" cannot mean what it did for the classical empiricists, who made it the equivalent of sense data. What is required is that larger view that has become current in our own day, according to which "experience" may be defined as the whole range of the self's active relationships with the other.

Self and Other are the two poles of experience. They are inseparable and correlative. The Self is never grasped independently of its interaction with the Other, nor can there be any discrimination of levels in the Self without a corresponding discrimination in the realm of the Other. Just as I grasp myself as a body only through my passive insertion in a realm of things that interact with me without taking "me" into account, so also my grasp of myself as a person is had only through the presence of other persons who do appeal to "me" for a unique response. I am a thing only in relation to other things, and a person only in relation to other persons.

If my experience were exhausted by these two levels of interaction, there would be no need to talk about God. The fact, however, is that it is not. For there is a dimension to experience not covered by these, a level of the self which transcends all its particular preoccupations. This is the level on which I find myself real over and above my involvements with any individual person or circumstance—a level from which, in a sense, I am called to pass judgment on all these particular involvements. It is the area of final responsibility which can suffer no encroachments, not even from those I love, if I am *to be myself*.

At this pinnacle of selfhood the correlative Other is God. I grasp myself as real over and above all my day-to-day forays into the world because I find myself appealed to above and beyond all these particular engagements. Unless a response were called for by One outside the immediate situation, my own reality would be limited to that situation. If it is not, it is because, more intimately than the people and things of my environment, and constituting me on a level which they do not reach, You too are present demanding to be heard.

To be a person is thus ultimately to be responsible in a way that calls all particular relationships into question. It is to stand in the presence of One to whom I am answerable for all that I do. Assuming this answerability, and maintaining this relationship in each event of my life, I accomplish myself as a person and confirm myself in being regardless of particular outcomes. By responding to Your appeal in all my dealings, I give body to Your presence in my life and lift that life to the level of the divine. On the other hand, to reject this relationship, or to let it be compromised, is literally to undo myself in whatever I do.

The experience of God thus grounds, and is one with, the experience of self. It is His nearness which first of all puts me near to myself and creates the inviolable zone which I am. Indeed, God is so near that I cannot fail myself without first failing Him. This is what Thomas More knew. It was the secret source of his strength. What he refused was not just the abandonment of his own convictions but, more radically, a betrayal of You that is identically perdition.

Human and Divine

One of the urgent needs of our time is to close the conceptual gap that exists between being human and being holy, between secularizing the world and sanctifying it, between man's creativity and his creaturehood.

There is much talk today about mankind's coming of age.

The secular thrust of contemporary culture is seen as man's assumption of final and creative responsibility for the shape of his life in the world. One writer inteprets this new stance as "the discovery by man that he has been left with the world on his hands, that he can no longer blame fortune or the furies for what he does with it." The achievement of a truly human society is a task for man himself. It will come about, not automatically or through the intervention of some kind of *deus ex machina,* but only in the measure that man creatively takes charge of things.

So far, so good. Few would have any quarrel with what is here affirmed. But, like every declaration of independence, this one too has negative overtones that require criticism. The inevitable conceptual tension between human autonomy and divine transcendence is being resolved by rejecting the latter's relevance. Man's "growing up" is being equated with emancipation from religious tutelage, his "standing on his own feet" with "going it alone." Thus we are told: "The epoch whose ethos is quickly spreading into every corner of the globe is an age of 'no religion at all.' It no longer looks to religious rules and rituals for its morality or its meanings." For increasing numbers of men, maturity and atheism go together. Man emerges from infancy ony by rebelling against God.

The root of this distortion is the fancied *opposition* between the human and the divine. Because God is "Other," He must be alien. Because man suffices, he must be alone. In Proudhon's words: "Humanity and divinity are first of all antagonistic." The only way man can be himself is to banish the Intruder. Or so it is thought.

Actually, far from canceling out or conflicting with humanity, the divine is what constitutes it. The human person is not closed within the order of the finite and determinate, but open to Infinity. His very nature as person is rooted in transcendence, an openness to Being itself. "Since this transcendence is not extrinsic but is intrinsic to man's being, not a dimension superadded to his life in the world but rather as the ground condition for its possibility" (Rahner), it is essentially involved in all that man does. There is nothing distinctively human, no perfection of man as man, that is not intrinsically structured by God's creative presence, or finally intelligible except as a response to it. If man exists beyond limits, if he is radically indeterminate and called to a real future, if he can move through facts to possibilities and creatively exploit these for the geniune enhancement of himself and the world, it is because he dwells in Being's light. Nor can he truly perfect himself without, by that fact, promoting God's reign.

What this means, of course, is that to deny God is implicitly to deny man himself, and, by the same token, to affirm man is implicitly to affirm God. Any and every realization of truly human perfection is at the same time an actualization and embodiment of man's relation to God and of God's presence in the world. It is indeed, an effective doing of God's will, an achievement of obedient service, in a way that merely confessing His name will never render superfluous, nor a mistaken denial of His Reality ever vitiate. The reality of our devotion to Him is the humanity of our dealings with His creatures. This is the element of truth in Feuerbach's thesis: "The true atheist is not the man who denies God, the subject; it is the man for whom the attributes of divinity, such as love, wisdom and justice, are nothing." Just as we really love God only *by acting* in the light of His presence (however nameless) and the difference it makes in our lives, so we truly banish Him only when we suppress that difference. But that difference, the divine difference, is precisely what makes us human.

All this is not to suggest that express acknowledgement of the Transcendent is itself superfluous or that we are not called to sing His praise. One can indeed argue that only a knowledge of God can save man from worshiping idols and undoing himself in the process. But our point is simply this: Really to be human is, in a true sense, already to be holy; really to respond to the world in terms of its own inherent values is already to sanctify it; really to explore and exploit creatively the endless possibilities the divine presence opens up to us is already to be God's obedient servant and intelligent creature, man.

God and Community

In the last part of *The Phenomenon of Man,* where Teilhard takes up the psychological possibility of a genuinely universal love, he makes the comment: "As such, the collectivity is essentially unlovable. That is where philanthropic systems break down. . . . It is impossible to give oneself to anonymous number. But if the universe ahead of us assumes a face and a heart, . . . then in the atmosphere created by this focus the elemental attraction will immediately blossom." The remark is crucial for Teilhard's theory about the future course of evolution. It is also able, I think, to throw light on a problem that is troubling many people today.

For a new kind of doubt is presently assailing the religious conscience. It is not the familiar and haunting misgiving about

God's existence. In a sense it goes even deeper. What is called into question today—even by persons who accept a divine revelation—is the meaning and relevance of belief itself. Just what is gained for the world by explicit adherence to God? What of significance is added to a man's life and work by his cult of the extra-mundane?

Underlying this restless questioning is a new sense of man's temporal vocation. For contemporary man, time and this world have come into their own. They are no longer, as it were, mere preliminaries to the main event; they help to constitute it. Time is not simply duration, the continuance of what already exists, a span given man to prove himself worthy of heaven. Time is the creative process itself, in which the real is coming to birth. And the world is no mere stopover on the way to somewhere else. It is the very stuff of man's life, asking to be shaped by him and shaping him in its turn.

Thus, whatever ultimate meaning life may have, this much can be said already—life is a call to share in the world's making. It is a chance to intervene, to contribute, to enhance what exists by the sheer power of one's own presence and activity. In the same way, whatever the other ingredients of moral goodness, no man can lay claim to it who shirks his responsibility to the people and things around him or who, through preoccupation with rewards and punishments in the next life, virtually withdraws from this one. One cannot be good simply by avoiding evil. To be indifferent or apathetic to the needs of one's neighbor, to stand aloof from a world begging for help, is already to be guilty.

This awakening of man to the creative possibilities of this life and to his here-and-now responsibility for achieving an ever more human world has occasioned a new wave of religious skepticism. For there is the widespread feeling that traditional religions, with their emphasis on extratemporal salvation and the rules for reaching it, have served to distract the mass of men from wholehearted commitment to enhancing the present scene and really meeting its needs. In this view, the "religious" person is too much like the pathetic figure of Marcher in James' *The Beast in the Jungle,* whose constant preoccupation with what-is-to-come prevents him from ever coming to grips with what-is-at-hand.

Moreover, even if religion is not incompatible with a genuine commitment to this world, there is the further question about what, if anything, it adds to it. For just as science does not need the support of philosophy (with which it was originally confused) to make progress in its own domain—indeed, only when it broke loose from philosophy did it really begin to move—so also, many would argue, a program of human brotherhood can get along quite well, maybe better, without its traditional theological underpinnings. The theological dimension, it is felt, adds a needless source of friction in an area demanding wholehearted cooperation.

In the face of these misgivings, Teilhard offers a simple but powerful suggestion. Not only, he says, is God's presence among men the ontological root of their present aspirations toward unity and universal love, but explicit recognition of His presence is a necessary pre-condition for the realization of such love. For the unity of persons as persons is a function of the direct relation of each to the one Absolute—a relation that provides the ground of each person's dignity as an individual and yet, as shared, is the very basis of fellowship. Except as explicit response to a Personal Other "who stands in the same mutual relation to every member of the community" (Macmurray), genuine community cannot even be thought, much less actually intended.

The relevance, therefore, of religion to the human dream is that, through its institutions, it embodies God's presence in our midst as the ground of our personal union with one another. Religion is the institutional basis of universal communion. This is its business and what it is about. If it often seems like something else, the reason is that in too many "religious" hearts it is fear, not love, that reigns.

V.

Teilhard's Personalized Universe

THERE are not a few thinkers today who believe that we are going through what might be called a "crisis of the personal," both on the theoretical level and on the practical level. The older images in terms of which we tried to understand the world in its fullness, images based on considerations of the mechanical and organic realms, have broken down. In their place, the image of encounter has taken the center of the stage. We are beginning to understand that the wholeness of interpersonal encounter constitutes the most comprehensive point of view from which we can seek to understand the world around us. Such, for example, is the theme developed by John Macmurray in his two volumes of Gifford Lectures on *The Form of the Personal*. According to Macmurray, "All meaningful knowledge is for the sake of action, and all meaningful action is for the sake of friendship." The problematic of interpersonal relations provides the comprehensive framework in the light of which everything else must be understood. Failure to achieve a way of thinking the personal will mean failure to achieve a way of thinking reality itself in its integrity.

The crisis of the personal, however, is not confined to the realm of theory; it exists very much on the practical level as well. Anyone vested with any kind of institutional authority is tremendously aware today of the tensions under which he is forced to work. For today has witnessed the emergence of a new ideal, the ideal of personal authenticity. Due to the pressure of this ideal, which has captivated the minds of men everywhere, and which holds almost exclusive sway in the minds of the young, there are no existing institutions that are not being subjected to the most searching kinds of criticism. The tension between the individual and the institutional is fast reaching the critical stage. Unless a way is found for readjusting their relationships so that each domain is given its due, it is not inconceivable that the present course of development will lead to chaos.

Teilhard himself has signalized the centrality of this crisis of the personal. If up to now all of man's efforts to achieve a genuine unity have broken down, if the collectivities that have been realized are more akin to anthills than to instances of true brotherhood, is it not possible, he asks, "that in our theories and in our acts we have neglected to give due place to the person, and the forces of *personalization?*" Teilhard thinks so, and I think so. And in order to support this stand I should like to develop four points. First, the theoretical and practical aspects of the problem itself of the personal; secondly, the contribution which Teilhard makes toward its solution; thirdly, the metaphysical presuppositions of Teilhard's position; and fourthly, an indication of its ethical implications.

THE PROBLEM

The problem of giving due place to the person in our thinking and in our action is not simply the result of an oversight. If the person as such tends to be neglected, it is because focusing our attention upon him is a matter of extraordinary difficulty. Why this is so can be quickly indicated.

It has become something of a commonplace to speak of the person as transcending nature, that is, as transcending the objective and determinate structures by which he is situated in the world. The idea is central, for example, in the thought of Gabriel Marcel. This philosopher distinguishes three stages in human development. First of all there is the stage of *existence*. This is the stage in which man is, as it were, passively immersed in his surroundings, with his relationships to the environment more dictated by instinct than by choice. Secondly, there is the stage of *objectification,* in which man's initial participation in the world is broken down and fragmented through the process of language, thought, reflection, articulation. In this stage man becomes aware of himself as standing over against his environment, with his life placed in his own hands, a problem that he himself must now resolve. Finally, there is the stage of *being* which is the goal of personal endeavor. It is a stage of communion, of a new and human participation in the all-encompassing real, a participation that we must freely and personally achieve. As resulting from a kind of conspiracy of freedoms, this final stage inevitably transcends whatever objective structures may be required to support it.

Erich Fromm is another who sees the person as transcending the determinisms of nature. In his little book *The Art of Loving,* he portrays man as having become detached through consciousness from the world around him and involved now in the task of seeking a new and human oneness with it. This task is the task of love, the task of overcoming separateness imposed upon man by his very constitution as a person. In like manner, Max Scheler in *Man's Place in Nature* portrays the person as a being who has emerged from his environment and become objectively aware of it. Personal conduct is not simply a matter of reacting to stimuli subjectively experienced. The person is open to the other in its otherness. He is present to both objective facts and objective values and is able freely to proportion his activities as a response to them. It is this transcendence of man over the merely determinate and matter-of-fact that is the basis of his ability to introduce novelty into the world. Man's future is never simply the prolongation of his past. It is fundamentally a matter of freedom.

This, however, is precisely what creates the problem. For how can we think freedom? How can we think in a determinate way a being that is essentially indeterminate and open to a real future? Any kind of reflection that limits itself to exploring the determinate structures in nature manifests itself, by the same token, as radically incapable of handling the person. Hence, the fumblings of empirical science when it comes to the question of personal values. As Macmurray points out, science is able to chart patterns of continuity, but is helpless to deal with genuine initiative. Hence, too, the awkwardness of much of Scholastic thought when it tries to deal with the person. For although the Scholastics recognize that man as person is open to the Absolute and Infinite, they fail to exploit this insight when it comes to the moral realm. According to the Scholastics, man's vocation is to conform freely to pre-existing patterns, not to move creatively beyond them. His responsibility is limited to realizing law and order in his life. That he is responsible for the law itself does not seem to have occurred to them.

Thus, in the problem of thinking the person, the failure of modern scientific thought and of much traditional philosophic thought is one and the same. It is a failure to get the person as such in focus. The person who transcends determinate structures is nevertheless thought of in terms of them. In contemporary philosophic thought, however, the problem is sometimes reversed. For modern philosophers have zeroed in on the person. Existential phenomenology has penetrated in a profound way to the dignity and reality of the subject as such, of the person, of freedom. It sees in the person a kind of creativity that constantly projects itself beyond the determinate structure of the situations in which it finds itself. Instead of being ignored, therefore, the transcendence of the person becomes a dominant theme. Here the problem is not one of focusing on the person but of relating what has thus been focused upon to the rest of reality. Whereas traditional thought tended to sacrifice the person to cosmological considerations, contemporary thought stands in need of cosmology. For, if the person is so different from the world in which he finds himself, how understand him as having roots in that world? Are we left with a radical dualism between spirit and matter? And if we are, how can we understand the temporal origin of the person in the world or begin to define his place in the world?

These theoretical problems have their practical aspect as well. The practical problem of personhood is likewise connected with the person's transcendence over the determinate structures of nature. Here, however, nature must be understood as comprising not merely the order of psycho-physical determinisms but that of social determinisms as well. For it is man's new-found awareness of his transcendence as a person over the order of social institutions and social habit that is creating a good deal of the bewilderment presently besetting him. On the level of action, the problem of the person is that of knowing what he should do, what is expected of him. It is the problem of reconciling the creative vocation of the person with his status as a being under law. In the past, man understood what was expected of him in terms of the place he occupied in the social framework. If, however, as we have suggested, the person transcends the social framework, whither should he look for the guidelines of action? Whereas simple submission to existing patterns does not do justice to the dignity of the person, a simple disregard for them would seem to lead to chaos. This is the practical dilemma confronting contemporary man and the anxiety it has bred is felt on every level of society.

The Contribution of Teilhard

The contribution which Teilhard makes to the solution of the problem of the personal takes shape in his effort to discern the future course of evolution. His general question is: Where do we go from here? The present situation has resulted from the progressive synthesis of the elementary stuff of the universe along two complementary lines. The outward increase in complexity of structure has been accompanied step by step by an inward increase in centreity and consciousness. The term of this whole process has been man himself, the most complex of all creatures and the most centered as well.

But if man is the end product of evolution, must he also be thought of as its consummation? Must the stage we have already reached be viewed as constituting the final chapter in the history of the universe? Teilhard says "no." All the signs point to the fact that we are on the threshold of a radically new development. Just as in the past, the pressing together of elements on the level of spatial arrangement and organization (the tangential level) has always been the occasion of the emergence of a new synthesis, so also now in the case of man. What we witness today is a continually mounting pressure for the totality of the thinking units of the world to unite in a new way. Because of a variety of factors—for example, the sheer increase in numbers, the prodigious extension of the influence of each individual as a result of modern means of communication, the very roundness of the earth which prevents an indefinite outward expansion—the units of mankind are becoming tangentially interrelated in an unprecedented fashion. Nor is this interrelation a mere matter of external association. The birth of reflection has in addition provided the human phylum with an outer binder or envelope that prevents its branches from separating off and welds them together instead into a single whole with a common fate.

In an ever more intense way, therefore, mankind is coming to constitute a single and densely packed field of interrelated and interacting forces. Yet, as always in the past, ever more complexity means ever more consciousness. The kind of synthesis among men which we are witnessing on the tangential level cannot but herald a new "leap forward of the radial energies along the principal axis of evolution." A new and critical threshold in the evolutionary process has been reached. A veritable *mega-synthesis* is on the verge of being born. Since, however, the birth of this mega-synthesis will depend on man's free cooperation, it is important for him to understand its requirements.

One requirement is obvious. The mega-synthesis cannot be achieved unless the selfishness and egoism of individuals and special groups is held in check. In this connection, a rather transparent temptation presents itself. For since in man an element emerges that begins to live *for itself,* it might be thought that advance lies "in a line continuous with that initial emancipation." Segregation, aloneness, would be the path toward an increase of being, toward superman. Salvation would be achieved at the extreme limit of individualization.

That such tactics of isolation, whether it be the isolation of the individual or (what is more amenable to rationalization and therefore more insidious) the isolation of a privileged group, constitute a temptation can be seen from the fact that they ignore an essential phenomenon—"the natural confluence of grains of thought." Indeed, not only do such tactics ignore the facts already described that point to a common fate and a common destiny for mankind as a whole; they *also* contradict the fundamental lesson to be learned from the past. As the past bears out, consciousness is always the effect of union; every advance of consciousness results from synthesis, not from separation.

Granted, therefore, that evolution is groping toward a synthesis of mankind as a whole, that the human element can achieve himself fully only in active relationship and oneness with the rest of his kind, the question arises as to the shape that this new synthesis will take. In answer to this question, Teilhard makes two observations. First of all, progress toward this new unity cannot dispense with external organization. Progress in consciousness is the correlative of greater concentration and arrangement on the tangential level and cannot be had without it. But this arrangement, this organization—and here we have the second point—must be such as to preserve what has already been achieved. The passion for unity must not be allowed to suppress or submerge the level of consciousness already attained in the person. Only if the organizational arrangements are such as to allow persons to be fully and freely themselves can we really speak of progress and not instead of retrogression.

Here, however, is precisely where man's attempts so far to

unite have failed. Organizational attempts at present seem more like a process of materialization than of interiorization. Instead of achieving a new level of consciousness, persons are being lost in a new matter. In place of a new freedom, we have the regimentation of totalitarianism or the enslavement of the individual to the machine. The person, who is an original center reflecting the universe as a whole in a unique and inimitable way, is being treated as a mere functional element in a gigantic organism.

If this is not to be the case, if universalization or *totalization* (as Teilhard calls it)—this achieving of a new unity—is not to sacrifice the elements that are uniting, then a new path must be found, a path in line with the fundamental drive that has animated the universe from the beginning. This path, Teilhard insists, is the path of love. Love alone, as testified by daily experience, "is capable of uniting living beings in such a way as to complete and fulfill them, for it alone takes them and joins them by what is deepest in themselves." The union of love differentiates what it unites. It personalizes by totalizing.

To be sure, to conceive love in this way is not to conceive it in merely sentimental terms. For Teilhard, love is the fundamental cosmic force that runs up and down the whole evolutionary scale. It is the fountainhead of cosmic energy. What we perceive when we "go down into the internal or radial zone of our spiritual attractions," is not something limited to man but is absolutely universal. For, as Teilhard remarks, "if there were no internal propensity to unite, even at a prodigiously rudimentary level—indeed, in the molecule itself—it would be physically impossible for love to appear higher up, with us, in 'hominized' form."

Love, therefore, in its deepest sense, is that basic affinity of being with being, that drive toward synthesis, which has characterized and moved forward the whole evolutionary process up to now. "Love in all its subtleties is nothing more, and nothing less, than the more or less direct trace marked on the heart of the element by the psychical convergence of the universe upon itself." What man, then, is called to do is to give full play to this fundamental energy in his life. What has been implicit in evolution up to now must become explicit and thematic. The synthesis toward which man is moving will be truly progressive only if it is a synthesis of love, only if it is the work of a universal love.

At this point Teilhard raises a difficulty whose solution gives access to his central insight. The difficulty is simply this. Is a universal love really possible? "Man's capacity, it may seem, is confined to giving his affections to one human being or to very few. Beyond that radius the heart does not carry, and there is only room for cold justice and cold reason. To love all and everyone is a contradictory and false gesture which only leads in the end to loving no one."

As Teilhard himself admits, this objection has real force. Common sense is right. The collectivity as such has nothing particularly lovable about it. This is where the philanthropic systems break down. It is impossible, he says, to give oneself to anonymous number. But, he goes on, "If the universe ahead of us assumes a face and a heart and, so to speak, personifies itself, then in the atmosphere created by this focus the elemental attraction will immediately blossom. Then, no doubt, under the heightened pressure of an infolding world, the formidable energies of attraction, still dormant between human molecules, will burst forth."

What Teilhard means, I think, can be put this way. No love

105

that is genuinely universal is possible unless it has a universal focus. This is why Teilhard looks to the universe ahead of us to personify itself. It is not, of course, a question of the universe becoming a person. The personification of the universe consists rather, as Teilhard himself explains, in its "charging itself at the very heart of its development with the dominating and unifying influence of a focus of personal energies and attractions." This is the point. Persons can be united in a personal way only if they are united around a personal focus.

For the unity of persons as persons is not that of an organism, all of whose elements are functionally interrelated. Nor can it be conceived on the model of a universal form in which numerically distinct individuals participate. The unity of persons is a unity of free initiatives; a community of uniques in their very uniqueness. What is distinctively original about each person is his capacity to give a unique and free response to value. Personal fellowship, on the other hand, is based on the fact that the capacity of each person to respond is ultimately directed toward one and the same supra-personal absolute value. The unity of persons as persons, therefore, is a function of the direct relation of each to the Unconditioned, to *Omega*. Except as explicit response to this Supra-Personal Other "who stands in the same mutual relation to every member of the community," genuine community cannot even be thought, much less actually intended.

Conversely, to actualize a love for this universal and transcendent focus is *eo ipso* to actualize a love for that whole realm of which it is the focus. I cannot truly love God without extending my love to all those to whom He stands in the same mutual relation as He does to myself. For Teilhard de Chardin, therefore, progress in evolution will depend on our thematizing the religious dimension. The multitude of men will be able to achieve the unity to which they aspire, a unity which will not submerge the person but exalt him, only if the driving force toward this unity is an explicit love of God and an explicit recognition of each man as a child of God.

So much for Teilhard's doctrine on the requirements of mega-synthesis. What I would like to do now is to apply these fundamental insights to the problems with which we started, to the problems, namely, of the person. What light, first of all, does Teilhard's doctrine shed on a metaphysical understanding of the person both in his originality as a person and in his relatedness to the world? Secondly, what light is shed on our understanding of the contemporary ethical situation of the person?

Some Metaphysical Reflections

There are two key ideas in Teilhard's doctrine of the personalized universe that we have outlined. The first idea is the absolutely universal and transcendent character of love itself. It is as driven by the forces of love that the fragments of the world up and down the scale "seek each other so that the world may come to being." The second key idea is the essential relationship and openness of the person to Being itself, to the Absolute. Only by bringing his life into active accord with this fundamental relationship is the person able to achieve himself as a person. And this achievement of the person is, as we have seen, precisely the achievement of a genuinely personal community.

To express these two key ideas in ontological terms, that is to say in terms of *being,* is our purpose in this section. If, however, our ontology is not to betray these fundamental insights, then the notion of *being* must be stripped of all purely passive and static connotations. "Being" as we are using it here is not a mere matter of *actuality* or *givenness*. It is not "being" as something affirmed but rather as affirming itself. It is "being" as act, source and center of activity. It is, in Tillich's terms, being as the *power of being*. In this sense, *to be* is always *to be for being,* to be promotive of being, to be a love of being. As Tillich has pointed out, love and power go together. It is being's devotion to being that is the ground of its power and the source of its creativity. It is, indeed, as absolute and infinite devotion to being that God is creator of the world.

From this point of view everything that exists exists as a participation in power. Each existent, from the rudimentary particle to the person, is an active capacity to promote transcendent value. Each is an active source affirming in its own way the whole of reality and bringing it toward completion. The particle, to be sure, is affirmative of the absolute value of being only implicitly and indirectly. By affirming itself not in isolation but only in relation to what is outside itself, it takes, as it were, the first step toward wholeness. It manifests its *being-for-being,* for what is absolute and comprehensive, by entering into syntheses with the other than itself (the tangential level), syntheses which, precisely as more comprehensive than the original elements, exist as new and higher powers of being (the radial level). In the person, on the other hand, the promotion of being itself becomes explicit and thematic. Open to the Absolute, and constituted a person by his relation to it, the person looks to a synthesis that is absolutely comprehensive. There are no limits to the person's horizon. There is nothing that lies completely outside or beyond the range of his affirmation. His vocation is to achieve in his life a synthesis without limits.

In these terms, both the continuity of the person with the rest of the world and his own distinctive originality can be understood. Not only is the person, like everything else in the world, an instance of being's power; the person is moreover a concrete synthesis of all those powers beneath him. If unlike everything else he stands in direct relation to the Absolute so that he hangs, as it were, from above, immediately and individually on God's creative power, he also and at the same time has roots that reach downward to the very foundations of the world. If he is truly God's child, he is also in a profound sense the world's as well, an issue of all that has gone before, a synthesis achieved in time of all those energies and powers which below him exist only fragmentarily.

The person is thus continuous with the world and yet reaches beyond it. In him the power of being to affirm being is unleashed absolutely. He is, like God Himself, a love of God Himself. He is not limited to interaction with finite others but can welcome the Infinite itself into his life. He looks, indeed, as Teilhard suggests, to the achievement of a universal community, a community which will have God as its focus and in which each person on the basis of his love for God will be lovingly related to every other person.

So it happens that Teilhard's doctrine of the universe in the process of personalizing itself, and Tillich's idea of being as power, are marvelously in accord with one another. The combination of the two themes provides, moreover, a way out of the embarrassing impasses which previous thought about the person has so frequently encountered. The notion of being as power, as the power to be for being, to love being, to promote being, leads us out of the essentialism that we saw characteristic of much Scholastic thought. It leads us out of the closed world of fixed and static forms into the open one of process and development where individuality, interaction, encounter and creativity become dominant themes. On the other hand, the downward extension, *à la* Teilhard, of this notion of power into the realm of things helps us overcome the radical dualism characteristic of so much of existential thought. For things are not primarily and immediately objects of knowledge, constituting a kind of inert spectacle for contemplation. They, too, are centers of activity, spontaneous powers, with which the self precisely as self, that is, as agent, is dramatically engaged. With the primacy of action over knowledge thus restored, the possibility of genuine novelty in the world is reintroduced. Nothing, therefore, prevents us from taking that novelty which is the person as the culmination of a long process of interaction rooting him in the world, rather than as some kind of inexplicable interloper.

All this is not to say that we now have an adequate metaphysics of the person. The full implications of such a conception have still to be explored. They do, however, look promising and they do, moreover, throw some light on the problem of action confronting the person in today's world. To this practical problem we now turn.

SOME ETHICAL IMPLICATIONS

The practical problem confronting the person is that of knowing what he should do. As we have suggested, this problem is especially acute today because of the contemporary emphasis on transcendence and creativity as defining characteristics of the person. Modern man has achieved a new awareness of himself as a person. He sees himself as, in a real sense, reaching beyond all that is merely matter-of-fact. Not only does he transcend the order of psycho-physical determinisms, he transcends that of social habit as well. Just as in the past he was judged to betray his personhood if he ceded to a life of instinct, so now the same condemnation is levelled against him if he merely accepts the social order he finds and makes no attempt to better it.

The question therefore arises: Where look now for indications of what is expected of him? In the past, such indications were largely supplied by the societal framework in which he found himself. Born into a settled and determinate way of life, he knew pretty well what he was supposed to do. If these indications are no longer to be considered final, if they are starting points rather than end points, then the person would seem to be left completely to his own devices without any norms to guide him. Such at least is the conviction of those who are doggedly fighting to maintain the force of traditional moral codes. They feel that if the absolute binding force of traditional norms is in any way relaxed, then man's moral life will quickly degenerate into a simple matter of subjective caprice.

There is, of course, much to be said for this position. It would indeed be true without qualification if beyond the realm of determinate structures there were nothing at all, if man's moving beyond these structures meant moving into a kind of void. If that were the case, then man's only choice would be between chaos and conformism. But the whole point of our foregoing considerations is to indicate that there is another alternative. Beyond the realm of fixed patterns there is the patternless by excess. Beyond the realm of particular and determinate beings there is, not nothing, but Being itself. And it is, I suggest, man's

111

openness to Being itself, to Omega, an openness that constitutes his very nature as a person, that will provide him with all the guidance he needs for a genuinely moral life.

The point at issue, therefore, between opponents and defenders of traditional natural-law theory is not the question as to whether or not there will be norms. The point at issue is much more profoundly what is meant by the word "nature" in this context. For example, is it the nature of man, viewed as but one determinate structure in a non-systematic manifold of interacting forces, that is to be our guide? Or is it man's nature as a person, open to the Absolute and called to resolve rationally and intelligently, that is, in the light of this openness, the moral problems constantly arising from the inevitably conflicting claims made upon him in the field of action?

If nature is understood in the first sense, not only is man's moral life reduced to a matter of conformism, but man himself, by being forced to ignore the possibilities which his presence to Being opens up to him, is inevitably condemned to do violence to his own intelligence. If, however, we take nature in the second sense, then, far from leaving the person to his own devices, we are on the contrary setting him the task of fulfilling his vocation as a person. Instead of putting him on his own, the second notion of nature enlists him in the service of Being, in the service of God. What is required of him is precisely that he spend himself in the promotion of Being, in the positive enhancement of every situation in which he finds himself. A task like this, to be sure, cannot be accomplished by ignoring the determinate structures of what one encounters. A determinate state of affairs cannot be improved unless the facts of the situation are first of all taken into account. But taking facts "into account" does not mean leaving them as they are. They are not mere occasions for resignation but challenges to our intelligent love. Not the world as it is, but the world as it yet may be, the world as love can make it, *this* is what should be guiding our steps along the way.

Such, I think, is the conception of morality to which Teilhard's personalism invites us. It is not a morality of mere conformism; neither is it one of chaos. It is precisely a morality of creativity, or better, of creative responsibility. In all his encounters with the things around him, man is called on constantly to respond to the call of Being, of God Himself, who seeks an ever fuller presence in the world He has made. That this increase of God's presence, this promotion of Being, can be achieved only if we give ourselves to a life of selfless love Teilhard himself has beautifully pointed out. His remarks, I think, provide a fitting conclusion for this paper.

"The longer I live, the more I feel that true repose consists in 'renouncing one's own self', by which I mean making up one's mind to admit that there is no importance whatever in being 'happy' or 'unhappy' in the usual sense of the words. Personal success or personal satisfaction are not worth another thought if one does achieve them, or worth worrying about if they evade one or are slow in coming. All that is really worth while is action—faithful action for the world and in God. Before one can see that and live by it, there is a sort of threshold to cross, or a reversal to be made in what appears to be men's general habit of thought; but once the gesture has been made, what freedom is yours, freedom to work and to love."

PART THREE

RESPONSE

In a world of emergent sense, rules (like ideas) are prospective, and are tested by what they lead to. Since the other is always new, encounters cannot be rehearsed. Hence, habits must be kept provisional.

There can be no settling down with past ways, no complacency over past achievements. What we need is to learn to listen, to let the other be other and meet him on his own terms, to trust that genuine meetings will generate new and richer meanings.

But only the discovered self can do these things—only the self that has cast out both fear and fascination with the immediate, and committed itself to integral humanness. Such a commitment is the root of morality. The moral decision is the one we can stay with, the one we can approve in the light of all its conditions and consequences, the one that fits in with life as a whole.

In our search for the right and thoughtful response, we arrive at old virtues seen afresh: at hope, which releases the other's healing powers; at love, by which we are first made whole; at faith in a Beyond to everything determinate whose challenge is always new.

VI.

Learning from Experience

WHEN we say to a person: "Be reasonable," we normally do not mean: "Stand pat." Being reasonable is not the same as sticking to one's convictions regardless of the facts. The word for that is stubbornness.

The reasonable (or rational) man is the one who allows himself to be guided in his actions by the reasons (*rationes*) inherent in the things with which he deals, by the rationale of the situation in which he finds himself. Whatever ideas or theories he may bring to a particular task, he is willing to let these be modified by what comes to light in actual practice. He is willing to learn from experience.

Experience is sometimes described as "the best teacher." We also hear it said, however, that learning by experience is learning "the hard way." As usual with popular maxims, both of them point up a truth.

Experience is the best teacher because, in the last analysis, it is the only teacher. Only in experience do we actually engage the real; only in experience is reality itself disclosed to us. Our ideas and our theories are not the real itself, *in person,* as it were; they are at best the real as *thought about.* They result from our effort to formulate the natures and connections revealed in action. We make this effort because we want to put ourselves in permanent possession of what is disclosed, to link it up with other disclosures, to provide ourselves with a map, so to speak, of the world we live in and so be better equipped for our "journey through life." In short, we think in order to act better. But we shall act better only if the map is accurate. The validity of our theories rests on their conformity to what is disclosed. If, unexpectedly, they lead us into a swamp, the map should be revised.

Even a poor map, however, is better than no map at all. And this is where the other maxim comes in. For man may be presumed to have learned something from his experience over the centuries, indeed to have gathered by this time a pretty good idea of what it is all about. The traditions which sum up this past are therefore standard equipment for an individual charting his course. The person who dispenses with these and insists on working everything out for himself is indeed a person bent on doing it "the hard way."

Yet even if willingness to revise a map does not mean doing without one, the question can still arise: Are all the map's indications ultimately open to revision? Are there no absolute truths? The answer, I think, is: there are. But if there are, it is not just because I think so, nor because I would be lost without them. Nor is it because, besides experience, there is some other basis for truth. (Note: Even my unquestioning acceptance of revelation is based on my encounter with Christ and His Church, that is, on the experience of faith.) There can be absolute truths only because, in addition to particular features, experience also discloses its own conditions of possibility. An absolute truth is a statement of such conditions. When the statement holds, it does so because what it asserts is really available (to a person paying attention) in any and every experience.

Robert Morley has written: "I don't think anybody learns anything from experience except, possibly, caution." Caution, indeed, we do learn. For unlike the real in theory, the real in experience talks back. But if the real can correct us, can actually show itself other than what we had previously thought, then its lesson is not merely caution. The fact that something talks back means also that we're not alone. It means that our lives are not finally imprisoned within the circle of our own ideas but can be, if we like, as wide as the world.

Openness to experience is openness to the Truth as it comes and speaks to us in person. This is *the truth that frees*. The reasonable man is the man who is willing to listen.

The Bias of Love

The idea is widespread that personal bias is out of place in the search for truth. A person, it is thought, should hold himself neutral until the facts are in and then commit himself only when forced by them. As Bertrand Russell has put it, the reasonable man is one who always proportions the degree of intensity with which he holds his various beliefs to the amount of certifiable evidence already available for each. To commit oneself without prior proof, or more than such proof warrants, is an abuse of reason. Oddly enough, Catholic insistence on the rights of reason has sometimes been misinterpreted as endorsing this "ideal" of the cool intellectual.

At the risk of raising cries of "subjectivism," I would like to make two points. The first is that the uncommitted thinker is a fiction. The second is that a certain personal bias is actually a prerequisite for knowing the real as a whole.

All thought takes shape against a background of bias because all thought is personal. Thinking is an activity, not of pure minds, but of persons—persons already involved in a world and caught up in the drama of history whose course they have helped to shape. Prior to taking thought, each has already taken action, concretely orientated himself in one way or another to the world and reality as a whole. This is what Josef Pieper means when he argues that there is no philosophy except in a religious context. The religion in question may be atheistic, the personal stand presupposed by reflection may be one that shuts out God, but it functions as faith none the less. Nor should it be overlooked that Russell's ideal of reason is as much a prior commitment as any that one could find. It assumes without proof that the world is more spectacle than theatre of action, that everything worth knowing can be known apart from love.

But if all thinkers are biased, what happens to the mind's ability to know the world as it is? What happens to thought's objectivity?

First of all, it should be noted that there is a realm of the real that imposes itself on us regardless of our personal likes. It is the realm of things and structures, the area of the impersonal. The impersonal not only exists independently of the person, it is indifferent to him. Bearing no relation to the bent of his will, exclusive of the person in the uniqueness of his freedom, it shows itself the same to all comers. To know it, love is not needed, only observation.

This indifference to personal bias, however, this lack of concern for *me,* which makes the impersonal seem the very model of objective reality, likewise betrays its partialness and the ultimate inadequacy of the spectator-approach to the real. For, since the whole of the real is necessarily inclusive of *me,* that whole is not thinglike but personal. I exist not as an element in a structure, but as response to an appeal. Addressing itself to me in the uniqueness of my personhood, the real cannot be known apart from the answer which I give.

And here lies the fault of the cool intellectual. It is not that he is personally biased, but that his own brand of bias is crippling. Remaining aloof until the claims of the real have been publicly validated, withholding his "yes" until it is wrung from him, he has already in effect said "no." He insists that the whole be approached like the part, that it force him instead of inviting him, and in so doing he shuts himself out. It is not the bias of detachment but the bias of love that is called for. The responsiveness born of love is not needed to make the real be (it does not destroy objectivity), but rather to let the real be on its own terms and to let it be for me.

For all its transcendence, the real as a whole can disclose itself only to eyes that *will* see and ears that *will* hear.

Living Contingently

To be contingent is to exist only by contact with what is not oneself—a contact which is often a collision. It is the opposite of being self-sufficient, self-contained. For us this means exposure to and dependence on the continuous influx of the genuinely Other, an Other that is always newly erupting into the tidy worlds we build for ourselves, rendering them outmoded before we have fairly gotten used to them and forcing on us the challenge to achieve new meanings and new syntheses.

This can be a painful business. The plaintive note in Burns' line about "the best laid plans of mice and men" finds an echo in the heart of each of us. How difficult it is to have to dwell in uncertainty, to have the outcome of our earthly hopes and schemes always dependent on factors beyond our control. How trying to see them, as so often happens, dashed to pieces on the unexpected, the unforeseen. And so we witness the tremendous efforts of our own technological age to seal man off from the unreliable, to enclose him in a world of his own making, one he can count on.

And yet there is danger here, too. As philosophers like Gabriel Marcel have warned, a world completely subject to man's control is a world cut down to man's size. It is a world without novelty, without surprises—no good ones as well as no bad ones. Since everything that happens in such a world follows a pattern of rigid determinism and is simply a working out of what is already there, it is a world without a future. Moreover, it is an impersonal world, a world in which only the functionary fits but in which the person has no place. When reason is rampant and technology becomes technocracy, the world it builds is no world at all.

What this means is that contingency, for all its aches and pains, is something to be embraced and lived rather than eliminated. If contingency is the impact of the Other on our lives, it should be remembered that only in conjunction with that Other can our lives have wholeness. To eliminate contingency, to try to construct a world that is simply a projection of ourselves, of our own private hopes and dreams, is really to try to eliminate all that is genuinely independent of us—all that

122

we actually need for our completion. For the wholly subservient cannot truly enrich. Only what confronts us with a sufficiency of its own can lift us out of our littleness and make up for what we lack.

To live up to his possibilities, therefore, a man must "live contingently." He must open himself to the genuinely Other, an Other that continually comes to him but whose coming is always a unique event, never wholly predictable. More than the workings of reason, such a life demands courage and love. For it is not a life whose structure is an abstract pattern, determined and fixed from eternity, which reason can find readymade. Its structure is rather one of encounter—an ever ongoing exchange whose meanings do not pre-exist but grow and develop as the exchange proceeds, and depend on the love that is brought to it.

Reason, of course, still has a place. But its place is second and subordinate. Its function is not to stand outside life and prescribe beforehand what must be the case. It cannot create the real. If man is contingent, his reason is, too, and must wait on the real to disclose itself. Reason, therefore, will illuminate life, and not distort it, only if it functions within what it seeks to understand and adjusts its formulations to what life itself reveals. To be true to itself, reason, like man, must be open to the shock of events.

Contingency thus has its risks. But the greatest is not to face them. For contingent man (as for Christian man, too), it is the heart, not the head, that counts most.

Achieving the Real

A sense of reality is not easily come by; it cannot be had without effort. As Emmanuel Mounier once wrote: "Reality is not delivered to your door. It is to be found by going to look for it."

Why this should be so is not hard to see. Reality has the structure of an ongoing, free encounter. It is a continually-to-be-achieved relationship between myself and all the rest. This means that right from the start, at the outset of human activity, a certain distance is established between the self and the other. This distance is a necessary condition for freedom. Without it, the self would have no elbow room, no possibility for reflection or choice. It would be a mere thing among things, wholly absorbed by the complex network of infrahuman forces, and no self at all.

But if distance is essential to the human condition, it is a distance that is meant to be bridged. By giving play to our activities, it allows the synthesis between myself and the rest to be a free and human one. Unfortunately, however, the challenge is too seldom met. The interval that would humanize reality becomes a barrier dividing me from it—an unbridged chasm that separates me from the fullness I long for.

Since this fullness which is reality consists in the creative collaboration of self and other, the failure to achieve it can take a variety of forms. It may take the form of retreat—the escapism of a false intellectualism or a timeless institutionalism. Abandoning the other completely, I construct a world of my own where everything is tidy and tucked away and which I desperately try to believe is more real than the one I forsook. Thought turns into fantasy and action is for holding the line. Or, for the more pragmatic, it may take the form of aggression. Instead of building bridges, I wage a kind of war, aiming to overcome my separation from the other by overcoming the other itself and reducing it to a mere means for my satisfaction. On a small scale, this is the style of all those who are simply out for themselves (unhappily, their number is legion); writ large and institutionalized, it is technology become technocracy. Either way, the alienated pragmatist is no more successful than the idealist and a good deal less amiable. Finally, there are those who neither isolate themselves nor assault the other but seek, by a kind of regression, to recover a lost immediacy in which self and other are both submerged in the passing moment. Here we have the pursuit of *la dolce vita,* the desperate and despairing search for distraction.

The vice undermining all these maneuvers is that they are basically negative and defensive. They all represent a loss of nerve. Even the tactics of an aggressive pragmatism are in their root a holding action, distrustful of the future and seeking only to maintain or aggrandize what is already there.

But reality never looks back. Its very essence is a kind of creative restlessness that can be what it is only by continually incorporating the past into new and undreamed-of syntheses. The real is the always bright and fresh, the never-finished, since, always confronting the self, if he does not flinch, stands the other with a new appeal.

What is needed, therefore, is not timidity but a kind of generous abandon, an eagerness to sally forth. The other is not the enemy; the other is our ally, the future's harbinger. If fear has a place in the encounter, it is not to paralyze action and freeze us in the past, but only to warn us of novelty and stimulate the real adjustments which meeting the other requires. But the meeting is what counts; it is there that newness is born.

A sense of reality is thus inseparable from a genuine spirit of adventure, of welcome for the new and the strange. It means a readiness to improvise, a joyful willingness to help make what has never been and goes beyond all our plans. It is the sense had only by those who know themselves shaped in God's image and rejoice at their chance to share in the process of creation.

Iconoclasm

It is often remarked that contemporary atheism is more a humanism than an anti-theism. Today's atheist is less concerned with denying God than with sweeping away the false absolutes that block human development. If this is so, then atheism today is more an ally of belief than an adversary.

One of the most difficult things for man to accept is his vocation to continual reform. Despite all the talk today about man's openness to a future that cannot be spelled out beforehand but must be continually improvised, man is forever trying to nail the future down—to *prescribe,* before it has come to be, the shape it *must* have. He is forever taking particular ways of organizing his experience—ways he has found to be relatively reliable and, to that extent, truthful in the past—to be the only way and the only truth, and hence beyond criticism. He is forever forgetting that his own nature as intelligent, as open to the Real beyond the given, to indefinite and inexhaustible possibilities beyond the actually accomplished, forbids him, if he is to be true to himself, from ever settling for the world as it is instead of as intelligent love can make it.

What is true here in general is no less true in the realm of religious belief. Despite the fact that religious belief thematizes man's openness to a Transcendent that radically calls into question all his achievements, the same tendency to box himself in with routines, to let the past dictate the future—and this no matter how obviously inadequate to authentic human aspirations these past routines may be—operates here as elsewhere. The religious man suffers the same creeping sclerosis that mankind suffers generally. He, too, is forever confusing limited truth with *the* truth, customary ways of relating to God with the one and only way. Determinate objectifications of God's presence—objectifications that are necessary and indispensable for man to live his relation to God socially and historically—are absolutized in a manner that exempts them from criticism and practically identifies them with the Reality they were meant to mediate. Instead of liberating man for the service of God in the promotion of human well-being, they become idols that tie his hands.

The root of such distortions lies in man's passion for security. It is truly a frightening thing to be homeless, to have no fixed place to lay one's head, no familiar and cozy corner to which one can always retire. It is not surprising that man should prefer to settle down and fortify himself against the future than to be always venturing into the unknown. The only difficulty is that settling down means settling for less than the fully human. It means betraying man's native vocation, which is to be always a pilgrim. It means stifling the call of Transcendence, which continually comes to man wherever he is and bids him move on into a strange country.

Such a betrayal of his nature occurs whenever man makes an idol of his institutions or considers any of his ways as beyond reform. It is especially shocking, however, when it is done in the name of God, when the very instrumentalities designed to mediate God's call become obstacles to hearing it, when all that is supposed to remind man of his distance from full humanity, and to stimulate his strivings toward it, becomes a roadblock instead, an excuse for staying where he is.

The fact that traditional religions have all succumbed in some measure to this absolutizing tendency is, I submit, beyond dispute. The fact that in so doing they have all in some measure separated man from his own nature and served to thwart human aspirations instead of promoting their fulfillment is likewise a matter of history. It is not that the religions have made no contribution at all to man's humanity. The charge—which serves as a kind of premise for today's atheist—is rather that, by clinging uncritically to past ways, they block further growth and obstruct what they once nurtured, And who will say that this is never the case?

Today's atheism, therefore, viewed as a wholehearted commitment to human development and as a rejection of whatever obstructive absolutism lurks in our religious traditions, is really performing an iconoclastic function not unrelated to that of genuine belief. Belief in God is incompatible with adherence to idols, with absolutizing any single aspect or element in man's life to the detriment of his full development. To the extent that the atheist can demonstrate, in his life, ways and approaches more conducive to human development than those proposed by believers, he does these believers a service for which they should be endlessly grateful.

Confidence in Life

One of the problems to which contemporary thinkers have given a good deal of attention is that of personal identity. Not "What is the world?" or "What is life?", but "Who am I?", is the odd sort of question they ask. It is an odd question because it makes one wonder what kind of answer is looked for or whether, when put in this way, it has an answer at all.

Just why this question should be asked so insistently today is, perhaps, not too difficult to discern. No doubt, it has to do with the wholesale process of change that we are presently undergoing. For it is impossible to be so thoroughly engaged in the task of replacing old patterns with new ones and not have one's confidence in the stability of any framework radically shaken. And yet a permanent framework in which they had a definite place and in terms of which they knew what was expected of them is precisely what gave individuals in the past their understanding of themselves. Take the framework away or call it into question and it is inevitable that the individual should then become a question to himself.

However this may be, what really bothers people today is not so much, I think, the question of identity as the question of existence. Not "Who am I?" (the question they constantly ask), but "Am I?" (the question they never ask), is actually the root of their anxiety. For, by an odd sort of paradox, the very moment we start focusing on ourselves is the moment we feel our existence slipping away. Just as the person whose attention becomes absorbed with the experience of love rather than with the beloved thereby weakens his capacity to love, so also the self who worries about himself instead of plunging into the world

129

around him has the least chance of *being* a self. If that is the case, however, then perhaps the best way of dealing with these questions is not to try to answer them at all but to turn our attention once more where it belongs—on the *other* beings that fill our lives and clamor for our recognition and response. Our self-awareness will take care of itself as soon as we once more become genuinely aware of others.

In this connection, a remark of Père de Finance is particularly suggestive. "Essential as the presence of others for us is," he writes, "nothing is more difficult for us to admit than that they really and truly *exist*." That is the crucial point, not our existence but theirs. We come to life with so many demands and so many fears that our demands will not be met, that the very richness of life escapes us. The people and things that surround us are mere shadows of themselves. We look to them, not in terms of their existential originality, but to see how they can serve our purposes. Our knowledge of them is not in terms of themselves but only as fitting into our schemes. As one wit put it, we know everything in general and nothing in particular. In place of real encounters, there is just a multiplicity of "crossed monologues."

If this situation is to be remedied, a new tack is called for. Since our knowledge of the world ultimately consists of our dealings with it, we can know it differently only as we deal with it differently. What we need is a new image, a new way of picturing and conceiving what it is we are about. Not *man-the-maker,* bent on making something out of life and seeing his environment only in terms of its usefulness; nor even *man-the-citizen,* whose life is one of obedience to laws and who feel threatened when the laws are questioned; but rather, as H. Richard Niebuhr suggests, *man-the-responder,* man engaged in a continuing dialogue with the concrete world about him—is the symbol we should employ. In this light, life becomes less a matter of realizing some distant ideal or of primarily looking to rules to guide our behavior, than the here-and-now effort to participate in an ongoing conversation.

Now, a conversation is not something all worked out before-hand. Indeed, if everybody comes to it with preconceived ideas about what the conclusion should be, it will never get off the ground. Again, if we may speak of such things as rules of conversing, their function is not to determine the outcome of the dialogue, but only to make it possible. The important thing in a conversation is for each participant really to *listen* to what the other is saying, to be aware of *being spoken to* and to make the *fitting response*. Nor will this be something he thought up beforehand; it will be that precisely which takes up the other's lead and moves the talk forward.

In life, as in a conversation, what we need is confidence in our own and the others' resourcefulness; confidence that by par-ticipating in it fully, we will learn something new, grow a little, and in the very process of enriching others, come away ourselves enriched.

VII.

The Search for Self

It is a curious paradox that the contemporary emphasis on personalism not infrequently results in exalting private and parochial interests over the common good. The ideal of service to others is subordinated to that of self-fulfillment. Having newly discovered his uniqueness as a person, the man of today is bent on keeping it in the forefront. He readily gives himself to direct personal relationships in which his unique value is acknowledged and taken into account. But the idea of submerging his personal preferences in wholehearted dedication to a common cause leaves him cool. His must be a personal contribution and one that redounds to him personally. He is reluctant to function anonymously as a mere cog in the organizational machinery needed for the attainment of large-scale goals.

In a certain sense, contemporary man is right. Personal life is inseparable from the exercise of personal responsibility. To be deprived of this, to have no say whatever in the disposition of one's energies, to be a mere tool in another's hands for executing designs that are not one's own, is the ultimate personal indignity. It is to be annihilated as a person, to become in the strictest sense a nobody. On the other hand, what institution can survive or what global end be effectively pursued if each man insists on the "right" *to be himself* and in all matters to follow his own counsel? Or to put it another way, is the contemporary emphasis on self anything more than a new and not very well-disguised version of plain, old-fashioned selfishness?

The fact that today more than ever before people are aware of their dignity as persons and resentful of anything seeming to slight or neglect that dignity is all to the good. But if this strong sense of what is owed to them is to be balanced by an equal sense of their own obligations, and this new self-awareness is not to degenerate into debilitating self-seeking, then another aspect of personal being, besides its uniqueness, should also be brought to the fore.

The human person stands in direct and immediate relation to the Absolute, to God. It is really this relationship that founds his dignity. But this relationship is not something passive. It must be continually affirmed in action and consciously lived if a person is really to be what he is. This means that a person falls short as a person if the horizon of his life is anything less than the Infinite. The Other to whom the self is correlative is not just this or that other, but the One who is present in every other and wants to be loved and served in them all.

To be himself, therefore, a person must be actively concerned with the Whole. Anything less, any kind of deliberate parochialism that has no eyes for what lies beyond "my own little garden," is really a failure to be.

Needless to say, devotion to this common good, to God's coming-to-presence in the whole range of the other, cannot be implemented without a certain sacrifice of individualism. For one thing, the common good will not receive more than lip-service if organized machinery is not devised to promote it. For a person's effectiveness in terms of direct personal contact is necessarily limited. If he is really to love God, he must be willing to insert himself in an institutional framework which, for all its indifference to his status as unique, nevertheless provides the means for widening his effectiveness and lessening the disproportion between the universality of his calling and his limited resources as an individual to reply.

Submission, therefore, to the impersonal discipline of organizational structure is not incompatible with personal dignity. If it inevitably implies a curtailment of personal decision-making in particular matters, it is itself a continual exercise of decision and responsibility in relation to the Whole. To keep the Whole in view is my calling as a person, and I am fully I only when I freely commit myself to its (not merely my own) realization.

The search for self is thus ultimately a search for God. Nor will the self be found until it is first of all lost in the wider perspective of a universal love.

Subjectivity and Social Process

The prerogatives of the individual subject are being absolutized today in a manner that cannot but subvert all rational process. The individual wants his own way or he won't play. The fact that this attitude assumes the guise of high idealism does not make it any less subjectivist.

Emphasis on subjectivity in recent years has by and large been a good thing. It was a needed reaction to objectivism inside and outside the Church. In secular culture, the experimental sciences were thought to provide such exclusive access to reality that anything beyond the reach of "objective method" became tinged with unreality. The whole realm of personal and moral values was thus separated from its ground in existence. Within the Church, on the other hand, excessive preoccupation with external structure and overemphasis on sheer conformity to rule conspired to stifle selfhood and render it suspect. Some reaction was called for. The reaction that occurred took the form of a reinstatement of the initiating, personal subject as that without which there would be no science and as that for which Church structures exist in the first place.

It is one thing, however, to make room for personal initiative and freedom in the realm of thought and institutions. It is quite another to isolate the individual subject and make it the supreme value. When this happens, subjectivism takes over. An individual's private views and desires become normative not only for his own actions but, supposedly, for everyone else's. Because I am ultimately answerable for everything I do, I alone have the right to determine what I shall do. Real obedience is irresponsibility. I may cooperate with the authorities when I happen to agree with their decisions, but I will not when I do not. To act otherwise is to betray my dignity and responsibility as a person. So, at least, runs an argument that is commonly heard.

The consequences of such absurdities are widespread. As can be easily imagined, they are playing havoc with religious life. In the name of subjectivity, there are no more "subjects." Everyone is on his own. But the chaos in civic life is even more disastrous. What Sidney Hook attacked as "uncivil disobedience" is being "justified" on moral grounds. Inequities in the system become not a challenge to correct it, but reasons for destroying it. "America is a house on fire," says one extremist. "Freedom now [that is, things the way *I* think they should be], or let it burn."

135

How promote subjects and avoid subjectivism? It cannot be done so long as personal responsibility is thought to preclude genuine obedience, or reasonableness is identified exclusively with "what I think." Instead of insuring the moral rectitude of my behavior, such a stance makes it impossible. For if morality means anything, it means not presuming to decide on my own about the justice and goodness of actions that affect others. The determination of the good is essentially a communal effort and presupposes on the part of all a willingness to submit to the requirements of community.

Obedience to legitimate authority is one such requirement. It does not, to be sure, guarantee the intrinsic reasonableness of my actions (nothing can guarantee that, although open and free discussion is a help). But obedience does make possible the insertion of my actions into a joint effort and alone assures their consistence with common life.

Since these are prerequisites for concrete morality, obedient action has a reasonableness about it that is *antecedent* and *extrinsic* to a consideration of what is prescribed. It is already a moral value commanding assent. An order, therefore, is not simply a proposal I am morally free to set aside if I do not happen to agree with it. By simply being an order, it already obliges me. Nor am I relieved of this obligation merely because what is ordered strikes me as unreasonable. The only time I have grounds for disregarding a command of legitimate authority is when, in my honest judgment, it contradicts something in the moral order that obedience is meant to serve. Hence, theologically, disobedience is always a turning from God except when obeying itself involves such a turning.

Subjectivity, therefore, is not an absolute value. It is essentially correlative to community. When it commits itself to the requirements of social process, its innovating capacity is a force for social reconstruction and reform. Only its contribution can forestall social sclerosis. But when subjectivity cuts loose from these requirements, it sinks into subjectivism and the harm it then does is more than subjective.

I Want My Rights

In a provocative essay on "Human Personality," Simone Weil remarks: "If you say to someone who has ears to hear: 'What you are doing to me is not just,' you may touch and awaken at its source the spirit of attention and love. But it is not the same with words like 'I have the right . . .' or 'You have no right to. . . .' They evoke a latent war and awaken the spirit of contention."

The cry for a greater justice is becoming ever more insistent and universal in our society. Often, however, the pursuit of justice is thought of only in terms of instituting pressures to have our own rights recognized. The emphasis is all on what others owe to us. We seem less worried, unfortunately, about what we ourselves owe to others.

The egoism of this orientation is reinforced, I think, by the individualistic conception of the origin of rights that one commonly meets. This is the idea that a man has rights prior to his contact with his fellows. He comes into the world, as it were, already endowed with them by his Creator. As Josef Pieper puts it: "Man has inalienable rights because he is created a person by the act of God, that is, an act beyond all human discussion."

137

The fact of rights is thus made prior to the obligations of justice. "Justice," says Pieper, "is something that comes second; right comes before justice."

This grounding of human rights on a source outside society is aimed at making them secure. If they depended on the will of men, they could be abrogated by men. Only, it is thought, if my rights arise independently of you, can I urge them against you.

Although the motive behind this theory is readily understandable, the theory itself is less so. For the existence of rights depends essentially on the reciprocity of persons. My creation by God gives me no rights at all in the face of impersonal nature. A tornado does not do an injustice if it deprives me of life. It is only because I am in your presence—you who are a person endowed with objective awareness and called by your native share in reason to respond to beings in terms of what they are and do—that the reality of my personal life first takes on the character of a claim or right.

My rights are thus founded on your obligation, as a *rational* agent, to treat me as a person. Rooted in *your* rational *nature,* they depend on your presence and are removed from your willfulness. No action of yours, posterior to your nature, can eliminate them—only your total absence. The act, therefore, by which a person first of all acquires rights is not his creation as a person by God but rather his insertion as a person in a society of persons. And this change of perspective has important consequences.

First of all, it highlights the essential tragedy of injustice. An injustice is not done by the mere fact that my reality as a person is ignored, or because something that belongs to me is taken away. For the whole of impersonal nature ignores my personhood and not infrequently by its inroads deprives me of what is mine. Injustice is done only because you who are obliged to be

138

responsive to the personal character of my being and activity refuse to be so. The injustice is in you.

This is the profound truth behind the Socratic idea that the doer of injustice is incomparably worse off than the victim. Because you are obliged by your very nature as a person to be responsive to me, you corrupt yourself in your personhood when you refuse the claim my presence makes upon you.

This interpersonal theory also supplies a positive content that is often lacking in treatments of justice. For my obligation to be responsive to you includes more than the duty not to hurt you or to correct only the hurts I have caused. It also forbids me to be indifferent to you, to comport myself in your presence as if you were not there, to pass you by as if you were some mere thing. Thus, simply coming upon you in a situation of distress, I cannot be unconcerned or refuse you reasonable help without equivalently negating your existence as a person. If I omit the response I owe you, I wrong you. I withhold something that, by reason of my nature as a person, you have a right to expect from me, something that is your due. Justice, and not merely charity, demands that I come to your aid.

Finally, this correlation between the existence of my rights and your nature as a person shows up the futility of seeking my rights apart from yours. Inattention to you in my search for justice makes justice itself impossible. It is simply another form of egoism which, as Simone Weil suggests, leads not in the end to justice but only to strife.

Rules and Decisions

The idea that our conduct should be governed by rules finds little favor today. Joseph Fletcher, in his *Situation Ethics,* entitles one section "Principles, Yes, but Not Rules." What he means, of course, is that anyone making a moral choice should get all the help he can from ethical maxims and inherited codes of behavior, but he should not let them be the final determinants of his decision. Since a person is answerable for what he chooses to do, his choices should be expressive of himself, of his freedom. And since his choices are aimed at meeting the needs of the situations in which he finds himself, he should let them be governed by those needs and not by any *preconceived* notions of right and wrong.

However anarchic such a position may sound, especially to the dwindling defendants of natural law theory it contains enough truth to merit attention. There is indeed a crippling oversight in the notion that the moral life is simply a matter of bringing our choices into line with pre-established moral principles. What such a view forgets is that the principles in accordance with which we are supposed to make our decisions are, in the last analysis, themselves matters of decision. A moral principle, directing me how to behave in certain circumstances, is not something that can be arrived at simply by studying either myself or the facts confronting me. A moral principle is a rule of action that, as such, is not something properly known at all but something freely adopted. To hold a moral principle is personally to subscribe to a view about the way things, not *are,* but *ought* to be. It is justified, therefore, not by what is already the case, but only by the consequences of putting it into practice, only by the effects of doing what it prescribes.

If this is so, then we can understand the objection of someone like Fletcher to the position that we should make all our choices in conformity with pre-existent principles. Since these principles are themselves matters of choice and decision, what this comes down to is that all our choices should be governed by the choices of others—that others, and not we ourselves, should decide what is good for us. In an age that is newly sensitive to the rights and prerogatives of individual freedom, it is not surprising that such a view comes under increasing attack.

But there is another side to all this—a side that those advocating the need for personal decision in moral matters in their turn too often overlook. Let me explain.

Every real choice is the actualization of one set of possibilities in preference to others. However implicitly, it is effectively (and in the most emphatic way possible) saying of what is chosen: "Let this be." It is subscribing to and commending its existence not simply from some limited perspective, but also absolutely. My very decision, in the circumstances confronting me, to do this rather than that is a practical declaration: "In circumstances such as these, this ought to be done." In other words, a genuine choice between alternatives always involves, at least implicitly, the adoption of a principle of conduct.

"Implicitly," I say, because often enough we don't explicitate the principles on which we are acting. Indeed, it is precisely the business of ethical reflection to make explicit what we are implicitly affirming by our behavior in order to see whether or not, when it is brought into the open, we can really stand by it. The basic question that has to be asked is: "Do I really want, can I really subscribe to, a world in which, for example, doing A in such circumstances is the rule?" If my answer is no, then however advantageous doing A may appear from a limited perspective, it

is not something that I can commend absolutely, nor, conse-
quently, can I commend the person doing it (myself included).
And to do it now—i.e., to bring into existence absolutely what I
cannot approve in the same way—is to put me radically at odds
with myself. It is to introduce that division within me which goes
by the name of a bad conscience.

Thus, if moral principles are really matters of decision, it is no
less true that moral decisions are really decisions of principle. If
we are going to act rationally, there is no getting away from rules.
A rule is implied in anything we knowingly do. And it has its
justification, moreover, not in the good intentions of the person
adopting it, but only in what its regular observance would lead to.

To be concerned, therefore, about rules of behavior is not to be
morally hidebound. It is an effort, rather, to bring out the full
implications of our choices and to see if, then, we still want to
make them.

A Matter of Character

Most of the contemporary discussion of morality is centered on
"crisis situations." What should I do in these very particular
and conflicting circumstances? Should I simply plot my course in
conformity with general principles? Or should I fix my attention
on the peculiarities of the immediate situation and try to meet
it as sincerely as I can? Those who hold for the "principles"
approach argue that only consistent application of universal
principles assures any kind of objectivity in the realm of morals.
Situationists, on the other hand, contend that a preoccupation

with principles involves such a blurring of differences as to be morally stultifying. In the heat of their debate, both sides neglect the very ideas that might help to resolve it—those old-fashioned ideas of habit, virtue and character.

The importance of "character" in ethical matters can be seen from this, that only as involving character is an act human and moral in the first place. The merely routine or the merely impulsive—except as manifesting traits of character acquiesced in by a person—are devoid of moral quality. Nor do they get such quality from the way they happen, in a particular case, to determine the environment. A moral act is first of all and in its essence an act of *self-determination,* that is, an act in which the agent, beyond merely exhibiting the dispositions he has acquired through past activity, newly ratifies or modifies them, and so determines the *sort of agent* he is to be in the future. In responding humanly to a particular situation, a person does more than shape that situation; he shapes himself. He "in so far commits himself not just to *that* isolated act but to a *course* of action, to a *line* of behavior" (Dewey). He reinforces or weakens a habitual orientation that accords (or is at odds) with the requirements of human life, and so sets up the conditions of his future moral career.

The trouble with situationism is that it forgets all about this career. The agent is thought of as atemporal, a kind of angel, natively endowed with all that is needed for right judgment and action, and completely unaffected by the weight in him of past experience. The freedom to act humanly becomes a given instead of something to be achieved. The good will needed for good action becomes a presupposition instead of what is at issue. While a pure spirit might approach a situation in this fashion, a creature of habit like man, whose past is always operative in the

143

present, deludes himself if he tries. This is why a moral decision can never be limited to meeting a particular situation in its immediacy. Just as my past, such as it has been, limits and qualifies my present power to act rightly, so my present action will inevitably affect my future capacity. Both the sort of agent I have been and the sort of agent I am to be—that is, the whole question of character—is involved in every decision.

The advocates of rule morality, however, are no less neglectful of character. They too are more interested in the goodness and badness of isolated actions than in the goodness and badness of people. Only here the goodness of an action is reduced to its lawfulness. It is not a matter, as with the situationists, of "meeting" a particular situation, but of insuring that a particular action is not in violation of some general and timeless precept. Morality so conceived is less concerned with the positive integration of the objective and developing context in which the person finds himself than it is with putting limits on impulsive activity. And individual freedom (because it is practically identified with such impulse) is something to be restricted rather than achieved.

Now, the point we want to make is that the notion of character would seem able to mediate between these two positions. As the personal achievement of a stable and fruitful relationship with one's natural and social environment, character is both individual and general, subjective and objective. It is the rational organization of individual impulse along socially beneficial lines; the acquisition of subjective dispositions that reliably promote the objective harmony of persons (community). A concern for character thus looks to the concrete without getting lost in immediacy. It is mindful of universal requirements, not as external limits to personal freedom, but as really its inner accomplishment. In short, it stresses what contemporary moralists so often forget, that moral goodness is primarily a perfection of persons, not of acts; that actions are good only in relation to the goodness of persons; that this goodness of persons is a matter of habitual dispositions that have to be worked at to be acquired. Only good habits make a man good. But good habits do not just happen. They must be cultivated.

Wholeheartedness

Underlying much contemporary talk about freedom is a presupposition that too often goes unexplored. It is assumed without question that all a person must do to increase his freedom is to increase his power, to augment his capacity for having his own way. The fact that the central problem of freedom is less a matter of *doing* what I want to do than of really *wanting* to do what I do goes unnoticed. That is why so many of today's struggles for greater self-determination end in disillusionment. The person who has successfully resisted the establishment and had things his own way frequently finds he likes them now no more than he did before. In fact, he often likes them less. For now there is no one to blame. He begins to see that the question of whose "thing" it is, his own or somebody else's, is ultimately irrelevant to his really wanting it.

This distinction between simply wanting something and really wanting it may sound curious, but it is also crucial. It underlies the perceptive remark of J. Giles Milhaven about freedom. Commenting on why some students failed in freedom even though they had been given free rein, he wrote: "As a matter of fact, they weren't that free. *They didn't fully want what they wanted*" (italics added). Since this is indeed the crux of the matter, it should be further developed.

There is, of course, a sense in which we always do what we want to do. Unless we wanted to, at least to some extent, we wouldn't act at all. But wanting in this minimal way is perfectly compatible with a measure of not-wanting. In fact, this is normally how we behave. We do things, but we don't have our hearts in them. We pursue a line of action, not because we ourselves find it inherently worth-while, but because other people expect it of us—people whose wishes we fear to oppose. Or again, we pursue it precisely because it's what they don't want. In this case, what we do is not important—in fact, it's often a bore; the important thing here is to have the upper hand, to be "our own man."

In short, we are continually making choices that we ourselves cannot wholly approve, choices that we know we wouldn't make were it not for extrinsic factors, and choices that, even as we make them, we also realize are at odds with our own other interests and desires. As a result, we are inwardly divided. There is inevitably an element of reluctance, of halfheartedness, of holding back, in our action. If it is true that we are doing what we want, we are certainly not fully wanting what we do. And this division within us, quite apart from external constraints, is enough to destroy freedom at its core.

The basic problem of freedom, therefore, is one of "wholeheartedness." It is not first a matter of overriding our opponents; it is a matter of integrating ourselves. Take away all restrictions, supply us each with unlimited means to execute our desires, and this basic problem would remain. Until we master the conditions

146

for integral wanting, for *being wholly* in what we do, freedom is at best an illusion. What, then, is needed?

The first thing needed, I suggest, is that we take our wantings seriously. For, in the last analysis, they ground the worth of things. Apart from our wants, things are without significance for us; they leave us cold. Taking our own wants seriously, however, is not the same thing as leaving them to themselves and indulging them as they arise. For the way they arise is piecemeal. They are simply reactions to present objects that, so long as they are not examined for their conditions and consequences, can never be more than fragments.

If our wanting is to be wholehearted, then what we want must be linked with the rest of reality. It has to be grasped not merely in itself, but in its connections, in what it portends for our life as a whole. This means taking thought. It means cultivating a habit of sustained reflection, of stepping back from immediate goods and enjoyments to see where they lead. It means refusing to endorse our initial reactions until their credentials have been checked and validated. For no one can really want to start what his mind tells him he won't want to finish.

The aim of thought, then, is not to suppress spontaneity but, through enlarging its scope, to guard it from short-circuiting itself. Its function is not to substitute for wants and feelings, but to liberate them from their fascination with fragments, to let them be reactions to more than the immediate. What we cannot approve reflectively—i.e., taking into account all its implications and con-sequences—we cannot fully want. And if we don't fully want what we do, our doing will never be free.

147

VIII.

The Virtue of Hope

HOPE is something of a forgotten virtue. In comparison with belief and love, it receives little attention from philosophers and hardly more than that in the lives of most of us. We seldom look to deepening our hope. We seldom think of hope as a disposition to be deliberately cultivated. Yet, as I shall try to show, hope is the fundamental response we owe to God and the basic condition for our own fulfillment as persons.

One of the reasons why hope is little esteemed is the ease with which it is confused with other things. Sometimes we think of hope as a kind of natural optimism. We picture the "hopeful" person as one with rose-colored glasses who goes around telling people not to worry because everything turns out right in the end. The truth is, of course, it does not. Only a little living is needed to know that things often go wrong, that our best laid plans not infrequently come crashing down on our heads. If we are worried, it is because we have reason to be. Somebody who tells us otherwise is either living in a fool's paradise or, at the very least, recommending a luxury we cannot afford.

Rejecting a false optimisim, however, does not mean that we entertain no hopes at all. Of course, we do. We may hope for a raise, or hope that an operation we have to undergo will be successful, or hope that our son will be admitted to college. We

148

have all sorts of hopes. But we do not think that having them makes us virtuous. And we are right; they do not. For, just as blind optimism is more a matter of temperament than of virtue—a temperament, indeed, that can easily lead us astray—so also particular hopes like these have nothing to do with virtue but are simply a matter of everyday desires plus a reasoned calculation of their chances of fulfilment. It is in this sense that we speak of youth as the time of hope. The young man hopes for a great deal from life—that is, he wants a lot and does not yet know his own limitations or the odds against him. Part of his growing up will be learning to trim his sails, to limit his desires to what he can reasonably expect.

But if hope is neither the blind refusal to face up to reality nor an attitude based on a hard-headed calculation of probabilities, how are we to think of it? We cannot practice it unless we know what it is. I think some insight into the nature and importance of hope can be gathered if we look at the way it functions in the area of personal love. In the realm of love a disposition is required that is neither blind optimism nor shrewd realism, but a genuine virtue whose name is hope. Let us see how this is so.

It is almost a cliché to say that love is a risk. To love another person deeply and genuinely is to put the meaning and happiness of one's life in that person's hands. When we love, we shift the focus of our concern and preoccupation from ourselves to another. The other's fulfillment and happiness are what we seek. Our very life becomes a gift and all we ask is that the gift be accepted. Whether or not it will be, however, does not depend on us. Try as we may, we cannot compel another to accept our love or make room for us in his heart. We cannot force love.

It is like a door at which we knock but which can only be opened from the inside. It can also be shut at any time. Thus even when a loving relationship has been established, there is no guarantee it will last. Since love depends on the freedom of two people, its existence is a continuous task at which one or both may fail.

To approach another with love, therefore, requires a heart filled with hope. The lover comes with a prayer, "Let me be with you"—and can only hope to be heard. He looks to a relationship that is meant to be forever, but can only hope that it will be so. Without hope, that is, a willingness to count on another's freedom as reliably for him, he would never take the step. Without hope, which embraces the whole of the future, his love could not even begin.

Needless to say, this hope which is involved in love has nothing to do with that naïve optimism described above. The optimist is a kind of determinist. He thinks that whatever he wants must automatically happen. The lover knows, however, that there is nothing automatic or inevitable about the relationship he seeks. He knows it comes as a gift that need not be bestowed, that is always a surprise. Again, because love is essentially free, the hope connected with it is not based on calculations. The lover may indeed realize that his love gives another person the power to hurt him, a power which that person would not otherwise have. He knows that betrayal is only possible where love has been given. But he does not think of this. He certainly does not base his hope on the chances he has of avoiding betrayal. In a sense, he does not base it on anything. He feels it rather as something which he owes, *something which has to be given for love to be possible at all*. Only if he is willing to rely on another's goodness and love, only if he hopes in him, therefore, can that person come near and heal his isolation. To refuse to hope is thus to render the other powerless to help us. To refuse to trust another is thus already to betray him.

Here we come to the heart of the matter. We sometimes have the idea that hope is a sort of hypothesis that has to be tested before we give ourselves to it fully, that we have to have special grounds for hoping in someone, but none for withholding our hope. Actually, the reverse is true. For the hope we are talking about is not an attitude or disposition appropriate only in special situations. It is not something we indulge in only when we think we have good reasons to do so. On the contrary, hope is that cast of mind and heart which a person must bring to life as a whole for the simple reason that *he is a person and is called to fulfil himself in a relation of love with other persons.*

What this means is that hope as a virtue is never *merely* a matter of *hoping for* something. It is never merely a question of something I want and hope to get. Right from the start hope is something interpersonal, a relationship between persons. To hope is really to *hope in you.* And what I hope for is not some particular good which I think will enhance my life. What I hope for is my very being and growth as a person. I *hope in* you *for* my salvation.

No one can be a person all by himself. Just as an infant is able to grow and develop at the beginning of personal life only under the loving care of the mother and within the warm circle of family affection, so all through our live we need the love and respect of other persons in order to be ourselves. And the reason is clear. If our lives are to have any meaning, then they must make some difference in the world around us. If it makes no difference what I do, then my life is meaningless. But, as a matter of fact, what I do in my personal life makes no difference to the universe seen as impersonal. The stones and the stars, the grass and the gritty soil are completely indifferent to my presence. They take no account of me. If they were all that existed apart from me, then being myself would be pointless.

Such, however, is not the case. Besides sticks and stones, there are also other persons. If my life makes no difference to a stone, it can make all the difference to another person. This is why I say that to be and function as a person is to be in relation to other persons, to find a home in the hearts of one's neighbors. Quite simply, I need you in order to be myself; I depend on you and hope in you to let me be, to give me room to be.

This is the real meaning of hope. Hope is not a matter of optimism nor one one of calculation. Hope is a willingness to look to other persons and to rely on their love for one's own coming-to-be as a person. That is why hope is a virtue. A virtue is a personal disposition enabling one to realize his destiny as a person. What hope enables us to do is *to enter the realm of communion* with other persons to which we are called. Without hope, we could never take this step. Unless we are willing to rely on one another, love is impossible.

From this standpoint, we can also see why hope is infallible, why it can never be a mistake to approach another with hope. This does not mean that we are never deceived in particular cases. We have all had the experience at one time or other of being let down by someone we trusted, someone in whom we had hoped. Christ Himself knew what it is like to be betrayed. But this does not mean we were wrong or foolish in hoping. It only means that the particular person on whom we relied has himself fallen short as a person, that he has declined the love which our trust in him made possible and has preferred to remain alone. Our hope was not a mistake, since it is, in a sense, something we owe to all. The mistake was his who freely chose to fail us and proved himself unreliable.

We thus never need a reason for hoping, although we may have reasons to temper or moderate our hope in particular instances. More precisely, we always have a reason for the general disposition of hope—a reason that is identical with our very constitution as persons—and, prior to any individual encounter, no adequate reason for not entering it trustfully. For, the personal self is called to communion antecedently to any particular relationship. His vocation to communion is not dependent on the particular persons he meets, but, as one with his own nature, is a pre-condition for such meetings. The person is already related to Being Itself and called to respond to Being before he is related to particular beings. And hope is simply the ratification of this original relationship and calling. Hope is that disposition of the person which allows the creative presence of the Other to function creatively in his life. It is the practical recognition that Being Itself is also Being-for-us, that God, in short, both in Himself and in the finite beings that mediate His presence, is love. Only in terms of this recognition, this disposition to trust the Other, can we begin to share in that love.

IX.

Love and Reality

AN understanding of the relation between commitment and knowledge in man's search for the real has become a fundamental need of our times. Man today is finding himself increasingly unable to commit himself unconditionally to anything. In place of an unreserved dedication of himself to truths and values conceived as absolute, he prefers the tentative stance of the "open mind" and the flexibility required for continual adjustment to an ever-changing environment. As one author has put it, "ultimate values [are viewed as] matters of extrarational personal preference, largely of the emotional or esthetic order, rather than of universally valid intellectual truth."

Factors contributing to the prevalence of this attitude are not hard to find. One of them is man's growing sense of time and of his own historicity. Formulations and institutions achieved in the past and hitherto regarded as absolute tend now to be seen as relative to particular contexts. This relativism, moreover, is reinforced by the practical annihilation of space brought about by modern communications. The individual man is no longer able to be nurtured within the comfortable security of a single tradition or isolated world-view that provides him with *the truth* about life and his place in the universe. From infancy he is bombarded by pluralism. The different traditions that in the past were spatially separated now confront him together in his living room and compete for his allegiance. Small wonder if the authority of each of them is thereby diminished and the powers of the individual to give himself wholly to anything are hamstrung by his confusion.

But perhaps the most important single factor is the rise of the "ideal of reason." Erected on the widespread esteem for science and things scientific that characterizes our age, this "ideal" would translate an uncritical grasp of "scientific method" into a way of life. In all matters, so it would urge us, "let us first examine the facts, and draw only such conclusions as the facts warrant. If no conclusion is warranted but some conclusion is necessary—since life does not wait on certainty—then let us hold the conclusion tentative and revise it as new evidence is gathered." As Bertrand Russell once put it, the rational man is one who always proportions the degree of intensity with which he holds his various beliefs to the amount of evidence available for each. The point is that in all cases our commitments should be tailored to the evidence on hand to justify them. Where there is no evidence, there should be no commitment. Until such facts are in as can compel our adherence, not commitment but neutrality and cool detachment are the order of the day.

Needless to say, admonitions of this kind have a certain appeal. There is the ring of tough-minded realism about them. What could be more reasonable than to wait on the evidence before deciding one's course? And yet it does not take much subtlety to remark that an unjustified prior commitment is at work behind the scenes. For not only do the proponents of this policy presuppose that the real is simply "matter of fact," settled and determined quite apart from the active intentions of the knower; they preclude by the very stance they have adopted, by their commitment to such a world, the possibility of knowing it in any other way. If one is to commit oneself only in proportion to the evidence on hand, then the only evidence one can have is evidence that imposes itself idependently of one's free commitment. To put it another way, if every gift of ourselves is to be a function of prior knowledge, then we are already committed (and condemned) to having only such knowledge as can be had apart from love.

And here is the crux of the matter. For, as I shall try to show, the real as a whole is not simply "matter of fact." Ultimately not thinglike but personal, it can reveal itself in its fullness only to one who is already open to it, who is biased in its favor, who has already freely committed himself in an attitude of loving responsiveness. And if this is so, then the "ideal of reason" is no ideal at all. Far from avoiding unwarranted commitments, the so-called rational man has committed himself with a vengeance. He has himself shut the door on all that approaches wholeness. By his very attitude he puts beyond his reach the possibility of ever attaining any thing like ultimate sense. He has imprisoned himself within the limits of a half-world. And it is not surprising if the reality he then confronts seems more nightmarish than real; if, however hard he looks, nothing appears within his chosen horizon to which he can give himself wholly.

But our purpose in this paper is not merely to attack this abuse of "scientific method." Our aim is rather to show positively how knowledge of the real in all its breadth is not independent of, but on the contrary is inevitably a function of, one's personal orientation. This will be our first and our major task. If we succeed here, then a second question will also confront us. For we will then have to see how knowledge so acquired can avoid the charge of subjectivism. Let us turn to our first point.

Knowledge of the Real Dependent
on Personal Orientation

I think a good beginning can be made if we first of all consider the distinction which Marcel makes between *subject* and *object*. There is, it is true, a variety of ways of interpreting the subject-object correlation, but Marcel's is the one which will be most helpful for our purposes.

Roughly, the distinction between subject and object is founded on the distinction between the personal and the impersonal, between person and thing. More precisely, it is based on the different ways in which persons and things enter our experience. Starting with the notion of thing, we may say that a thing is that which I experience as unable to take *me* into account. It is here before me. I deal with it in a variety of ways dependent on its structure. But in all these dealings and interactions it remains by its nature oblivious of *me*. The way it is inserted in a given situation, the way it reacts to the pressures brought to bear on it, all this depends simply on *what* it is, on its *nature*. The fact that it is *I* who am dealing with it means absolutely nothing to it. Anyone else dealing with it in the same way will get the same response. A thing, therefore, is grasped as a reality that is exclusive of me, one for which *I* do not count and in which *I* as such have no part. It is grasped as that which is the same for all comers. And it is its being grasped in this way that is referred to when a thing is described as an object.

With persons the situation is quite different. If all reciprocity is excluded in my relation to things, an element of reciprocity is part of the definition of my relation to persons. A person is that

157

which I experience as able to take *me,* precisely in the uniqueness of my selfhood and personal freedom, into account. A person is one whom I experience as able to *respond to me.* This inclusiveness of me in another's world, whether it be actual or only grasped as possible, is the touchstone of the personal and immediately and irrevocably separates the person from the mere thing. The fact, however, that the inclusiveness may (and, in most cases, does) remain merely possible means that as regards the person (unlike the thing) two types of knowledge are possible.

One type is like the knowledge I have of things. This is the kind I have when, for all my realization that the being in question is a person, I do not know him *in person.* What I mean is that the person is there, a part of my experience and my world, but not precisely as focusing on me or aiming himself in my direction. He is grasped as functioning in pretty much the same way as he would if I were not there or if someone else were in my place. I do not grasp him, any more than I would a thing, as being precisely a response to me. He is simply a being who is acting in a certain way because he exists in a certain way. He is acting according to his nature, which in this case happens to be personal. This is clearly the way I know most persons, not only those I pass on the street, but also all those with whom I deal simply in terms of a particular role or function. I know full well that the anonymous guide I approach for directions is a unique person, a center and source of free initiative, an embodied liberty. As someone has remarked, I would be frozen with horror if a car seemed about to run such a one down. For all his anonymity, he is not to me simply an *it.* But his liberty and unique initiative are reduced, as it were, to the status of abstract attributes, characteristics that can be, and are, just as well found in others. Al-

158

though these attributes are actually functioning here, and have to be if I am to grasp the other as a responsible person at all, they are not directly engaged by me nor present to me in and for themselves, but only as implicit aspects of a certain structured pattern of activity. It is the activity and its successful accomplishment, not the other in and for himself, that interest me here and hold my attention. And it is this subordination of the other to being an element in a structured pattern that precludes his being present at the same time as a reality in and for himself, one who gives me access to himself and includes me in his world. The reason why love and business do not mix is that they involve distinct apprehensions of the other person which are internally conflicting. The type of knowledge or apprehension of another that is apt for business purposes or for the aims of action in general is one in which he is grasped not in himself, in person, but in terms of his qualities, capacities and natural attributes. It is a type of knowledge which, while not making a thing out of him, is nevertheless modeled on our knowledge of things, of pure objects.

There is, however, another type of knowledge of persons. This is the kind we have when we deal with them not merely directly (as opposed to simply passing them along the way), nor merely as beings who are persons (as, for example, when we allow our recognition of their personhood to guide our activities in their regard), but as ourselves responding to a personal initiative directed toward us in the uniqueness of our own self-hood. In this case, the other enters my experience precisely as turned toward *me,* precisely as interested in *me,* and as one, moreover, to whose interest in me I myself am open and responsive. In other words, for the type of knowledge I have in mind, there must be a certain reciprocal openness, a certain

159

mutual self-giving. It is not enough for another person to be willing to engage me in my personhood if I myself have no interest in such a relationship and prefer to keep it one that is "strictly business." The overt gestures of such a one in my regard will be seen wholly from the outside, detached, as it were, from their source and as more or less irritating aspects of an objective transaction that would be less complicated and would run more smoothly without them. Instead of being the active embodiment of another's gift of himself to me, they become by my very rejection of the gift mere features of a situation to be coped with. On the other hand, if the other person does not of his own accord reveal himself to me as one who is interested in *me* (quite apart from those qualities or aptitudes that may render me useful for one of his projects), no efforts on my part can bring about such a disclosure. For all my own good will, he enters my experience simply as another one from whose personal world "I" am excluded, and therefore as merely another element, useful or dangerous, of the situation in which I move.

But say there is mutual revelation and self-giving; say that a genuine personal reciprocity is achieved. The other is turned toward me in the uniqueness of my selfhood and I myself, undistracted by plans or projects of any kind, hold myself open and responsive to his loving interest. It is at this moment that I attain him *in person,* find myself, precisely as a self, included in his world. It is now that I experience the other for all his otherness, as taking *me* into account, as enveloping and enfolding me, as giving me a share in his very life, in himself. At this moment, I am no longer alone, surrounded by people who ignore me and by things which cannot do otherwise. *I* am with *you.* I have access to you in your personhood, as *subject.* And, the startling thing, it is now for the first time that I truly experience myself as a person. For it is really only in *your* presence that *I* am.

I say this is "startling," but perhaps it is less so than at first might seem to be the case. For all it means is that, since experience is constituted by interaction with the other, the self can grasp itself only in terms of this correlation. What it is for itself, therefore, will in a true sense depend on what it is for the other. If the real in which I have part were completely indifferent to me in the uniqueness of my selfhood, if from the whole range of the other with which I interact there arose no appeal addressed to *me,* then in relation to the real my capacity to give a personal response and be *myself* would be a matter of complete indifference and of no significance. I, as I, would not be real.

This, I think, is the root of our need for love. I need you in order to be myself. It is also the source of love's creative power. In loving me you give me myself, you let *me be.* And this too is what lies behind the insistence of those writers who find in the I-Thou relationship something altogether special. The point is not that apart from the I-Thou relation there is no recognition of the other as personal. We have already seen how this is not the case. Nor is it that in such a relation a person is somehow mysteriously united with another "mind." The significance of the I-Thou relation is not that it calls into play some special process of knowing, intuitive or mystical. What is important about it is precisely the experience of *inclusion.* In the reciprocal relation of persons *as persons,* that is, where the attention of each is directed to the other in the uniqueness of his selfhood and freedom, each finds himself, precisely as *I,* taken into account by the other, by what transcends himself. There is no doubt but that even here degrees of intimacy are possible. A relationship like this can grow and deepen. It will have a history. But the point that philosophers who concentrate on it want to make is that only in terms of genuine personal reciprocity, whatever the stage of its development, does a person find himself included in and part of the real, and therefore real himself.

The world, therefore, will really be different depending on whether or not I approach it with love. It will disclose itself as a place in which *I* can be at home and in which *my* actions can be seen to make sense only if I am not deaf, but responsive, to the personal appeals that are addressed to me. And this brings us to the heart of the matter. For whatever final sense the world may be thought to have, it is not a sense that imposes itself regardless of my concrete intentions and orientation. If the real is judged to be ultimately impersonal, if the person with all his hopes and dreams is considered in the last analysis to be a purely private affair, an illusory epiphenomenon of matter, a freakish accident in the universe, this will not be because such an interpretation is forced on one. It can only result from the crippling bias of scientism. An approach which is suitable for part of the real—that part indeed which is impersonal, which does leave *me* out of account and is therefore the same for all comers and publicly testable—has been arbitrarily applied to the whole. What is accessible by this approach, even though it inevitably leaves the thinker himself beyond the margin of the real, is made equal to all that is. That alone is admitted as objectively valid which can be publicly validated. That alone is the final meaning— even if it deprives the thinker himself of meaning—which finally discloses itself to any and all, which requires no personal bias to be grasped. But if no bias is needed to see it, only bias accounts for its acceptance as final.

If, on the other hand, the real is judged to be ultimately personal, that is, if the person in the uniqueness of his freedom

162

is seen to be not a matter of indifference, but included in and comprehended by the real in its wholeness, then this too will not be an interpretation that imposes itself willy-nilly. It too will result from a bias, from a personal, prereflective orientation. In place of the bias of impersonal, scientific detachment, the bias of love will be at work. *For only by the prior commitment of love and responsiveness do I have access to the Other as inclusive of me.*

Any formulation, therefore, of the final sense (or lack of it) of the world always takes shape against the background of a free and prior orientation. Thinking is an activity, not of pure minds, but of persons—persons already involved in the world and caught up in the drama of history whose course they have helped to shape. Prior to taking thought, each has already taken action, concretely oriented himself in one way or another to the world and reality as a whole. This is what Josef Pieper means when he argues that there is no philosophy, that is, no thought aiming at an ultimate and comprehensive interpretation of the real, except in a religious context. The religious context in question may be atheistic, the personal stand presupposed by reflection may be one that shuts out God, but it functions as faith nonetheless. Just as much as love, it is a commitment prior to proof. The only difference is that, whereas love heals the breach introduced into reality by man's self-consciousness and his power to reflect, and restores the real in its wholeness to the thinker, any orientation short of love will confront a world in which the thinker himself has no place. In the one case, the commitment is justified (not beforehand, to be sure, but in the very course of living it) by the integrity of the experience to which it gives rise; in the other, it can never be justified, since logically it annihilates the one who makes it.

163

Reality a Matter of Freedom

Now the thesis to which this leads is that the real in its ultimate intelligibility is not just a matter of fact but more profoundly a matter of freedom. Let us examine this a little more in detail.

If we say that reality in its wholeness is the synthesis between *ego* and *non-ego,* between the self and the whole range of the Other, then clearly this synthesis is not something given (as already existing) to the thinker, but is rather something to be freely constituted, a task to be personally accomplished. By the time man starts to think, the human race as well as the individual, he has already transcended nature, emerged from that state of original oneness with his environment when his relationships with the Other were wholly passive, a matter of instinct rather than choice. By the ability to think, which is the ability to step back from one's surroundings, the primitive synthesis has been resolved into its elements. The individual is no longer simply part of a larger complex. He has become a self, a being present to himself and distinct from the world that confronts him. The conduct of his life has been placed in his own hands. How he relates to the Other is no longer a matter of course but a matter of decision. His life is now problematical. With the prehuman synthesis shattered by his very emergence as a person, he is called upon to replace it with a new and human one. Precisely as human, however, it cannot be automatic.

For example, instead of reinstituting participation in the Other on the new level of freedom which thought has made possible, the self may give way to the anxiety born of its isolation and seek rather a spurious kind of security in its very apartness. The

Other becomes a threat to be warded off. Seen as essentially hostile, it must be brought to subjection. And so the self devotes its energies to technology and the art of control. However, with the progressive reduction of the Other to the status of means, the self's own isolation is proportionately reinforced. Reality becomes incurably fragmented. In such a person's life, all the elements of a possible synthesis are present, but the synthesis itself is not effected. The negativity of approach which prevents the person from seeing the Other as inclusive of himself makes genuine synthesis impossible. The real as whole and absolute, which might otherwise have come into being, remains in this person's life unachieved.

More, however, is involved here than the possibility of failure. If reality in its wholeness is a matter of freedom, then it can never be accomplished once and for all. As a work of freedom, it is a task to be newly begun with the dawn of each day. Not only must the effort to dominate be abandoned. Participation in the Other as other (by which alone wholeness is achieved) demands an abiding respect for its claims, a constant attitude of responsiveness that is sensitive to each new appeal and ever ready to go out to meet the Other on its own terms as it continually comes to presence. For the wholeness of reality is not that of a system in which each element has its place. Nor can it be conceived on the model of an organism whose parts all function in relation to the whole. Such conceptions not only destroy the otherness of the Other by making it a part of the Same; they completely ignore the personal character of the one who is called to achieve a synthesis with that Other. The model for grasping the structure of the real as a whole is that of an on-going personal encounter, one in which through the mutual openness of love, genuinely new meanings continually come to light.

This, then, is the basic reason for denying that the real is simply matter of fact or that it can ever be something finally settled and determined. Reality is the continuing work of freedom because, in the last analysis, reality as a whole is communion. Small wonder then that it cannot be attained apart from commitment and resolve. Only the man who reintegrates himself with the Other through love can know the fullness of the real since only by love is that all-inclusive wholeness first of all achieved.

Reality Versus Subjectivism

So much for the first of the questions raised at the outset. Personal commitment is essential to grasping the final sense of the real. But what about the second question? How can the position outlined here avoid the charge of subjectivism? If not only my knowledge of the real but the real itself in its wholeness depends on me and is a function of my personal orientation, how can it claim objective validity?

In order to answer this question, we must first of all determine the meaning of objectivity. The "objective" is sometimes defined as that which exists independently of me. It is something "out there" which is no less real in my absence than when I explicitly attend to it. What such a definition means to exclude is anything in the line of a private fancy, a mental projection or hallucination. It is the sort of "objectivity" which things may be said to enjoy; their being and functioning do not depend on my personal point of view. Such, for example, is the objectivity of the real as studied by the physical sciences. By the same token, however, it is a notion of objectivity that is applicable to only a segment of the real, not to the whole. For reality as a whole is not something "out there" for me to survey. If it is not a private fancy or mental projection, neither is it independent of me in its being. Reality as a whole is necessarily inclusive of me, and of all that is most original and particular in me. It is even, as we have seen, dependent for its wholeness on my point of view, on my approach. If, therefore, it is also objective, another meaning must be found for that term.

The way we shall use the term here is one that is wider and more fundamental than the one just indicated. That is objective, we shall say, which does not exist merely for me, that is, which exists for the personal other as well as for myself.

That this usage is wider is not hard to see. For how do I grasp something as existing independently of me if not precisely by apprehending that it exists and functions in exactly the same fashion for others? What presents itself as identical for all comers proclaims by that very fact its independence of each of them. But "independence" says more than "objectivity." What manifests itself as independent of persons, as the same for any and all, is clearly something objective, that is, something that does not exist merely for me. By being the *same* for all, however, it also clearly manifests its fragmentary and impersonal character. It is something lacking in personal depth, unable at once to be other than it is or to take persons into account. Exclusive of persons, it is no more than part of the real, some small portion of God's creation, not the comprehensive whole. Hence the danger of restricting "objectivity" to what can be publicly tested, of equating it with the narrower notion of "valid-for-all." If only what is independent of persons has objective validity, then "objective" would apply only to elements of the real but not to the whole that includes them.

167

As we have defined the term, however, that danger is avoided. It can apply equally well to a reality inclusive of me as to one that is independent of me. Let us see how this is so.

Suppose, for example, you and I are deeply in love. Our love is something dependent on the freedom of each of us. Apart from my good will and yours, and without our reciprocal and continuing fidelity, it would cease to exist. Not only, however, does it depend on us; it does not exist as such for anyone else. Love is something that can be known only from the inside, only by those who share in it; *amicus est amico amicus.* Those on the outside have only signs to go by, certain behavioral patterns which might lead them to suspect or infer its existence. Even here, however, they may be mistaken, and in any case they cannot by these means know the reality itself. Here we have something which comprehends us both, interior to which each of us exists for the other, and which for all its meaning in our lives nevertheless in a profound sense exists only for us.

Is this love of ours something objective? If the first-mentioned criterion of objectivity were applied, the answer would have to be "no." There is no area less amenable to public testing than that of love. But for us who are in love, not only is that fact irrelevant; the very idea of applying such a standard borders on the sacrilegious. We know our love because we live it; we know it from the inside as a reality that is larger than either of us, that comprehends us both. And because each of us grasps it as existing not merely for himself but also for the other, we know it—quite rightly—as objective.

Here then we have an idea of objectivity that is adequate to our problem. Not only is that objective which is independent of either of us and the same for us both. That also is objective which, though dependent on each of us, nevertheless involves us both. A state of affairs embracing both me and you (or the personal other in general) is necessarily seen, if it is adverted to at all, as being not merely for me but for you (or the other) as well. A situation of harmony or strife is the same for all involved even though, in the latter case, only one may be to blame. For I can no more avert myself from you without finding you divided from me than I can be your lover without you being mine.

The fact, therefore, that the wholeness of the real depends on me and is a matter of freedom does not take away from its objectivity. The total situation to which my free actions give rise is not something private and subjective but, along with me, involves all the rest. My actions may be unwarranted and based on misconceptions—indeed, if they proceed from anything but love they will be—but that is not the point. So long as I fail, for whatever reason, to integrate myself with the Other, then the real as involving us both remains fragmented—and objectively so. If it does not manifest itself as a whole to me, it is because it has never come to presence as a whole in my life. As involving me and identical with that interaction of Self and Other which is my life, it does not exist as a whole. If, on the other hand, the wholeness of the real stands revealed, this will not be because it was there all along waiting for me to discover it, but only because by my free efforts in cooperation with the Other I have helped to bring it about. Commitment is thus necessary for knowledge of the real as a whole because it is first of all necessary for the existence of the real as a whole. A truly integral real cannot disclose itself until it has first been achieved.

The importance of this thesis for philosophy, which aspires to formulate the structure of total reality, is clear. But, as we remarked at the outset, it is equally important for the general conduct of life, especially in an age like our own. To put it as Blondel once did, a man cannot fill his mind with truth unless he first fills his life with reality. This, however, he will never do apart from his own free decisions.

X.

Belief Today

ONE of the most striking characteristics of modern atheism is its pervasiveness. It permeates the contemporary scene like the air we breathe. It is less (at least as I shall explore it) a fully articulated ideology than a mood or temper, a kind of lived presupposition, underlying contemporary man's efforts to come to grips with his world. Instead of being the conclusion of an argument, it is the implicit starting-point of a concrete way of life.

This is at least part of the significance of the recent flurry about "death-of-God" theology. Whatever final importance one may attach to the phenomenon, and however much the "radical theologians" differ among themselves, the broad, popular interest they have aroused bears witness to a widespread uneasiness and dissatisfaction with what has been known as religion. Instead of being meaningless on the face of it, the idea of God's death strikes a responsive chord in the hearts of a great many people, especially the young. The death of God would seem, as Vahanian suggests, to be a cultural event that has only to be pointed out to be acknowledged. Even were it unacknowledged, the feeling is abroad that religion belongs to the past and that, whether or not God exists, a preoccupation with Him is an impediment to a truly human life.

This is the point. Modern atheism is really a new humanism, bent on exploiting the potentialities of this life and stressing man's inalienable responsibility in this task. Hence its power and appeal. The negativity of getting along without God is only incidental to the driving and positive intention to live humanly. If modern atheism is aggressive, its aggressiveness is positively oriented. It is a full-scale campaign for a more human life with the accompanying notion that relying on God for this was, and remains, a mistake. Life can make sense only in the measure that man himself puts sense into it. To look to God for a happy ending is irresponsible superstition.

That such a mood should prevail to the extent it does would, I think, be impossible without the convergence in contemporary experience of two related factors: the living reality of belief as alienation, and the growing appreciation of intellect as creative. Neither, by itself, quite accounts for the present temper. As we shall see creative intellect need not be interpreted atheistically. A theistic explanation of it is not only possible, but seems to be called for. If the case seems otherwise to contemporary man, it is because the creative ideal has emerged in a religious context that was—and continues to be—largely at odds with it. What concretely passes for belief in our culture too often involves a repudiation of intellect, an alienation of man from his deepest reality and responsibility as shaper of the world. On the other hand, the recognition of such alienation for what it is had to await the emergence of creativity. It is only in the light of a more human alternative that the distortions of current belief stand disclosed.

In the following pages, I shall try to trace out some of the relationships between these two factors and their bearing on contemporary godlessness. Since I take human creativity as open to another interpretation than that given to it by atheists who tend to understand themselves as its sole champions, it may be well to begin there. In the end, we shall have something to say about the connection between today's brand of atheism and authentic belief. For it may well be that, as Vahanian has suggested, the true line of demarcation runs not between atheism and theism but between idolatry and iconoclasm (both of which can be found among believers and unbelievers alike). If that is the case, today's atheistic temper may be seen less as a threat to the theistic stance than as an opportunity and a challenge.

I.

However one may wish to interpret the fact, that is, whether or not one sees it as a call to atheism, there seems little doubt that contemporary man finds his relationship to the world newly meaningful. He no longer sees the world merely as a place where he is putting in time on his way to somewhere else. It is no longer a testing-ground for life beyond the grave. Rather, the world itself has become the locus of man's fulfillment. It offers itself as a challenge to the full range of his creative powers. It is a wilderness to be tamed, energies to be harnessed, raw material to be converted into a genuinely human abode. Contemporary man no longer feels compelled, through ignorance or natural piety, to leave things as he finds them and put up with what he does not like. What he does not like, he feels called to change. His lot is not one of resignation and conformity to the existing state of affairs, however haphazard or irrational. His job, as he sees it, is to bring order out of disorder, to elaborate a city of man in which the previously random goods

173

of experience are brought under control, made readily available, stable and secure. The accomplishment of this task is both his own and the world's consummation.

The possibility of man's taking this active stance toward his natural and social surroundings and assuming responsibility for them depended on a number of conditions. For one thing, he had first to overcome his myopic view of time. So long as he remained ignorant of the past, he was naturally inclined to view the prevailing order in his world, whatever its limitations, not as something achieved historically, but as original, eternal, and even divinely established. There was something absolute and sacred about the way things were—a conception which the Christian doctrine of creation actually tended to reinforce—such that tampering with the given was felt as a kind of impiety. But once it became accepted that the present shape of things, far from being aboriginal, is the issue and upshot of an endless series of accidental convergences—in other words, a "happening"—the sacred aura surrounding the given was dissipated. The patterns of nature and society were desacralized and, in principle, were opened to change.

Another related condition for the widespread unleashing of reforming initiative was the radical weakening of the grip of tradition on individuals, which modern communications brought about. The communications explosion has prevented any single tradition from holding undisputed sway over communities and individuals alike. The questioning insecurity it has provoked—especially in those exposed to it in their formative years—has made doubt and dissent both widespread and respectable. The individual, as ultimate source of innovation, no longer feels obliged to conform to "the universally accepted" because this, even in appearance, no longer exists. The intellectual climate is volatile. However prone to routinization man remains, and whatever the practical pressures for homogeneity in a mass society, there is a general openness and respect for new ideas and practices, an attitude that is itself a novelty in the history of man.

But the central factor contributing to man's newly creative stance toward his world—and the one underlying the afore-mentioned changes in perspective—is the rise and triumph of modern science. Nothing has so profoundly affected man's under-standing of the nature and role of his own intelligence as has the extraordinary success of his scientific endeavors. In the light of them, intellect can no longer be viewed as simply called to contemplate a real which somehow stands over against it, fixed and complete. It is itself involved in a process of real-ization, of giving reality itself a shape and direction it never had before. Rationality no longer means simply the capacity to recognize the reasons (*rationes*) of things and act in accordance with their requirements. It means even more profoundly the capacity to shape the reasons of things in accordance with the require-ments of intelligence so that reason can recognize itself in whatever it does. Correspondingly, the notion of meaning itself has been radically reinterpreted. Meanings have ceased to have the fixity of eternal essences. They have become temporal and dynamic. They are not originalities to which the mind can only conform, but eventualities in whose emergence the mind can actively conspire. They arise through the interplay of independ-ent (that is, not systematically related) centers of action whose potentiality for consequences, since it is a function of the endless variety of contexts into which they may be introduced, is in-definitely extendible. New meanings can, indeed, emerge by chance convergences. But once intellect is freed from its fascina-tion with the actual, and turns instead to the deliberate exploration of the possible, the novel can be systematically and fruitfully pursued.

Dewey describes this new understanding of intelligence in the following terms:

The old center was mind knowing by means of an equipment of powers complete within itself, and merely exercised upon an antecedent external material equally complete in itself. The new center is indefinite interactions taking place within a course of nature which is not fixed and complete, but which is capable of direction to new and different results through the mediation of intentional operations. . . . Mind is no longer a spectator beholding the world from without and finding its highest satisfaction in the joy of self-sufficing contemplation. The mind is within the world as a part of the latter's own on-going process. It is marked off as mind by the fact that wherever it is found, changes take place in a *directed* way, so that movement in a definite one-way sense—from the doubtful and confused to the clear, resolved and settled—takes place. *From knowing as an outside beholding to knowing as an active participant in the drama of an on-moving world is the historical transition whose record we have been following.* (italics mine)

I have quoted Dewey at length, since it would be hard to find a more accurate description of the contemporary *attitude* toward intelligence. Admittedly, Dewey's interpretation has not won general acceptance among philosophers. Nor could the layman be expected to articulate his experience in precisely this fashion. But it is, I contend, what he *experiences*. Whether or not he knows it, he *lives* this view of mind, and he finds it satisfying.

In a sense, the scientific and technological experience of our age has provided contemporary man on the level of concrete life and practice with something philosophers in general have so far been unable to come up with on the level of theory. Erich Fromm has said that the great (theoretical) problem of today

176

is the reintegration of man in his subjectivity and freedom with objective nature. Past philosophies have not managed to do this. They have moved from the objectivism of the ancients (where man is integrated with nature, not in his selfhood, but only as a *kind* of being), to the subjectivism of the moderns (where the self, when it does not swallow nature, remains isolated from it), through the half-way house of medieval philosophy (which emphasized the person only to locate his fulfillment *as a person* in his relationship, not to nature, but to God). But contemporary experience, which I think Dewey articulates well, has itself provided man with this integration. He now *experiences* himself as one with his world, not through objectivist conformity to its structures (which negates his selfhood), but through creatively transforming them (which gives him selfhood *in actu exercito*). At the same time that individual intelligence has been naturalized, the world has been humanized. There is a new at-homeness, a new wholeness, about man's relationship to his world—not that of a snug system, but rather that of an ongoing *encounter* between independent initiatives (somewhat like a continuing conversation), which is at once a continuous challenge to inventive intelligence and a continuous consummation to the parties involved.

It is this wholeness of contemporary experience that lies back of its immanentist interpretation. Contemporary man, for all the loose ends life may contain, does not feel obliged to look beyond it in order to make sense of it. Since, however, I have suggested that this new stance does not exclude a theistic interpretation, it may be well, before going any further, to sketch one briefly here.

II.

Man's call to creativity is identically his experience of personal transcendence. The fact that man aspires to transform nature, to enhance his world, to move on endlessly beyond wherever he finds himself, is one with the fact that his nature is not-to-have-a-nature in the same sense as other natural entities. He is not so immersed in nature as to be imprisoned by it. As Scheler puts it, he is not condemned to carry his environment about with him "as a snail carries its shell." He is open to more than the determinately actual, and can deal with things not merely in terms of what they are but in terms of what they may become, in terms of their possibilities. He is, therefore, not confined to the brute givenness of structures but is able responsibly to shape them. In a word, in his being and activity, man *transcends* whatever confronts him as actually patterned and determinate.

Because of this transcendence, an ethics conceived simply in terms of conformity to natural and social structures is necessarily inadequate. The fallacy behind much of the argumentation in favor of natural-law theory is that it mislocates the "nature" in question. The nature which can serve as ultimate norm for moral behavior is not that which confronts man as determinately structured; it is his own nature as a *reasonable* being, open beyond the given, and called to reconstruct it in accordance with the requirements of intelligence. Thus a natural-law ethic is viable only if it is at the same time an ethic of reasonableness and personal responsibility.

But the question is: What does such reasonable responsibility imply? For the opponents of such an ethic argue that there are only two alternatives, conformity to patterns or subjectivist chaos. Nor could one answer them if beyond the determinate there were nothing at all, if beyond the patterns there were not the patternless-by-excess. In much the same way, Tillich's first two levels of courage, viz. that to be *as a part,* which involves a loss of self (objectivism), and that to be *as a self,* which involves a loss of the world (subjectivism), would exhaust the possible alternatives if, beyond beings, there were not Being itself. In other words, an *openness beyond determinate structures* is inconceivable (that is, it is no openness at all) if it is not at the same time an *openness to what is* beyond the determinate. Nor is it enough to describe this "beyond" as the realm of possibility. On the one hand, possibility is rooted in actuality, and, on the other, the order of determinate actuality cannot, by itself, provide the (ontological) space and ground for its own negation and surpassment. The realm of real and indefinite possibility thus necessarily occupies the infinite distance between particular beings and Being. Real possibilities are projected in the combined light of the determinately actual and the Infinite. In short, Being itself is inevitably ingredient in man's awareness of his own creativity. It is in Being's constitutive presence that he judges what is required for the world's enhancement. If someone objects that it is rather in accordance with the nature and requirements of intelligence that these judgments are made, the obvious answer is Yes—provided intelligence is viewed as the faculty, not merely of particularity, but of Absolute Being.

From this point of view, the thesis of Proudhon, namely, that humanity and divinity are first of all antagonistic, that the only way man can be himself is to banish the Intruder, is simply false. Actually, far from being at odds with humanity, the divine is what constitutes it. Man's very nature as a person is openness to God. His very essence involves transcendence. "Since this transcendence is not extrinsic but is intrinsic to man's being, not a dimension superadded to his life but rather as the ground condition for its possibility," it is essentially ingredient in everything man does. All that is distinctively human, every perfection of man as man, is intrinsically structured by Being's creative presence and is finally intelligible only as a response to it.

An immanentist view, then, of human experience, based on man's new creative oneness with his world and the new wholeness which that has made possible, does not exclude a transcendental version. In fact, since the two are correlative, neither is really possible without the other. This does not mean that we call on God to fill up the holes in our lives or satisfy specific needs. The problematic in experience must be resolved—in the measure it can be—on its own level. Since God is and remains beyond particularity, He abides forever on the far side of whatever solutions to our human perplexities we reach or fail to reach. But He *is* the light which illumines our search and measures all our achievements.

III.

To say, however, that the reality of human creativity does not exclude the reality of God, that the contemporary ideal of creative humanism can be theistically interpreted, does not mean automatically that creativity is therefore compatible with theism as a way of life. For, as we pointed out, atheism today is less the conclusion of an argument than it is the premise for a style of living. The point is not whether the idea of God figures (as it does above) in a reflective interpretation of experience, but whether the referant of that idea is to figure in any way in the conduct of one's life. In other words, can the idea of God have a real significance in the practical order without at the same time cramping and distorting that order? Can theism as a way of life be both significant and not dehumanizing? Today's atheist answers these questions in the negative. Looking at the history of religion, the record of man's attempt to translate the idea of God into practical terms, he contends that, where it has not been a record of downright inhumanity, it has at least fostered attitudes and practices that not only fail to give human intelligence its due but that run completely counter to the development of such intelligence. The only times when this has not been the case is when religion has ceased to have practical import and become more a matter of lip service. But this last is simply hypocrisy and should be candidly confessed and eliminated.

Underlying atheist criticism of the religious record is a theoretical conviction that it cannot be otherwise. Putting it in its simplest form, one might articulate it this way: Only the determinate and particular can have practical relevance, and nothing determinate and particular can be absolute. To absolutize the particular is superstition and idolatry; to refuse to particularize the Absolute is to deprive it of practical bearing. Religion is therefore either dehumanizing or without significance, an impediment to human progress or a waste of time. Either way, man is better off without it.

Since this dilemma summarizes the main thrust of contemporary atheism vis-à-vis traditional religion, and since their growing awareness of this dilemma is at the root of much of the "agonizing reappraisal" presently going on within the Christian communities, Catholic and Protestant alike, it may be well to explore it a little more in detail.

181

The force of the dilemma stems from the fact that it makes use of the very notion of transcendent Being which Western man has employed to articulate his understanding of divinity. If, for example, as Rahner writes, the primary "locus" of Christianity is the "transcendental experience which penetrates our understanding and our freedom as the unthematic ground and horizon of our everyday experiences" and which has as its focus "the incomprehensible wholeness of reality at its very center," that "absolute and holy mystery which we cannot seize but which seizes us instead, by its own transcendental necessity," then it is clear that this constitutive presence of the Christian God can be reflectively grasped, *not directly,* but only through the mediation of signs and symbols pointing beyond themselves. Moreover, these reflective representations will be necessary if man is to deliberately and socially relate himself to this God, and avoid an empty transcendentalism which, looking upon the transcendent as something elusive and unutterable, "advocates a program of so-called boundless openness to everything in general together with scrupulous avoidance of a straightforward commitment to anything in particular." As Rahner continues, "These objectivizations [that is, in human words, in sacramental signs, in social organizations] of God's own divine self-giving, which seizes man at his transcendental source, are necessitated by the fact that man must live out his original nature and eternal destiny as an historical being in time and space, and cannot discover his true nature in pure inwardness, in mysticism, and in the simple dismissal of his historical being."

But then the difficulty arises. Either these objectivizations are confused with what they objectivize and are themselves given absolute weight, or they are not. If they are, religion is corrupted at its root. There occurs what even Christians are beginning to recognize as the unbelief of believers, a genuine atheism in their own midst. God is particularized and religion becomes a special domain. It consists in a specific pattern of behavior, with positive and negative elements. Conformity to this pattern is required if one is to be on good terms with the Supreme Being. Since this is what counts, a person may go through the prescribed motions (and consider himself a believer) without even holding that God exists. He behaves "religiously" just in case— as a kind of insurance policy.

But even if God's reality is held to, His particularity limits His bearing on one's life to the meeting of specific injunctions. Whatever lies beyond these is religiously neutral, that is, to be dealt with as if God did not exist. Hence there are whole areas in the lives of "believers" where their religion makes no difference at all, where they are, quite simply, atheists. On the other hand, in the religious area, that of divine commands and prohibitions, since it precludes any weighing of the merits of what is prescribed or forbidden in favor of blind conformity, they forfeit their humanity. They cannot behave intelligently, doing or avoiding something because of its inherent intelligibility or the lack of it; they can only behave slavishly.

This is what lies behind the atheist charge that objectivized religion inevitably involves an alienation from the human and creative. A particularized God is necessarily extrinsic to man, a kind of imposition from the outside. To bind oneself to such a God is to put oneself in bonds, to fetter oneself to a set pattern no matter what arguments can be raised against it. In this case, theism as a way of life is anti-human and atheism is a humanist revolt.

But suppose the objectivizations of God are not confused with the divine itself. Suppose they are taken simply as "mediations and signs of God's incomprehensibility," with their importance not in themselves but in what they make present to us. As determinate patterns and structures, these mediations are simply relativities. Only what they look to is absolute and that, as absolute, is indeterminate.

At this point, the other horn of the religious dilemma emerges with full force. For if only the Transcendent itself (and not as objectivized) puts an absolute claim on us, and if this claim is essentially indeterminate, then what practical bearing can it have on our lives? Once the objectivizations of God are relativized, are we not left simply with the absolute (but purely formal) demand to act intelligently in all circumstances? Can doing God's will ever be anything else than meeting the demand of intelligence? But then, why bother with all the religious paraphernalia? Indeed, there are good reasons for dropping them altogether. So long as the life of intelligent action is decked out in religious trappings, there is always the temptation not only to idolize these latter, but to attach a kind of divine importance to our own conclusions as well. Whatever course seems dictated by our intelligence, instead of being entertained modestly and as corrigible by future experience, will tend to be identified with the will of Being Itself, to become a kind of eternal law sanctioned by God, and so exclude further inquiry. Hence, it seems better to many to drop all talk of God and simply concern ourselves wholeheartedly with the ongoing process of "making and keeping life human." As Dewey puts it, if we need a faith, let it be "faith in the methods of intelligence," not as access to another world, but as a force for enhancing this one, the sole means we have for "rectifying and expanding the heritage of values we have received that those who come after us may receive it more solid and secure, more widely accessible and more generously shared than we have received it. . . . Such a faith has always been implicitly the common faith of mankind. It remains to make it explicit and militant." This recommendation is being carried out today.

IV.

From what has been said, it would seem that atheism as a way of life not only is compatible with a theistic interpretation of human creativity but can even be construed as demanded by it. Any effort to move theism from theory to practice seems bound to further estrange us from God's reality. That is why, as is often remarked these days, the atheist in his very atheism is, in a real sense, closer to God than those who "believe." If God is the ground of our humanity, He cannot but be authentically (even if only implicitly) affirmed in any affirmation of the genuinely human. By the same token, to the extent that what parades as belief diminishes or curtails our human capacities, it is just as really (however implicitly) a denial of Him.

The question then arises: Even if one accepts the existence of God, is not an atheistic humanism perhaps the only authentic way to serve Him? Is there anything to be gained, for God or man, by diverting out attention from human and secular affairs in an effort to focus it on Him? This seems to me to be the decisive issue, and one calling for much more thorough treatment than I can give it here.

There are different ways to approach the question just raised —perhaps none of them wholly adequate in isolation from the others. I have tried to show elsewhere that the inherent ideal of the personal is a universal community of persons which can be conceived (and actually intended) only as a response to a transcendent Initiative. In other words, the common recognition and celebration of God's reality is a prerequisite for the full realization of personal life. I have also suggested (along with many writers, to be sure) that only the communal acknowledgement of the Transcendent can keep man from worshipping idols.

The point I would like to make here is that theism, not merely as a theoretical interpretation of experience but as a concrete way of orientating one's life, as a way of existing, is necessary if the humanistic ideal of creativity is not itself to become distorted. For, ingredient in the notion of creativity is the idea of man's own responsibility for the shape of the world. As Vahanian points out, far from proposing itself as something easier than the Christian ethic, the present-day atheistic ethic lays agonizing stress on individual responsibility and decision. But, then, what does this responsibility entail? Does it mean simply the assumption by man (individual? collective? both?) of the governance of his own life? Can one avoid aspects of responsiveness and answerability inherent in the notion of responsible behavior, or not ask the question: To whom is one responsible?

When God is eliminated as ultimate focus of one's practical orientation, it would seem impossible to keep creativity from degenerating into either a kind of Sartrean subjectivism or a levelling collectivism. If intelligence is simply a private endowment, then in my efforts to meet its requirements, I am answerable only to myself. If it is, on the other hand, essentially a communal affair, so that it is in terms of common approbation that its determinations are validated, then we do indeed move beyond subjectivism—the individual is now answerable to others, to the group—but we also fall under the tyranny of "what is commonly accepted." In other words, it would seem that only a thematization, in practice as well as theory, of the responsive and responsible openness of intellect to the Transcendent Other as its own ground can save the ideal of creativity from falling into either of these traps.

A practical recognition and celebration of God's presence to us need not mean diverting our attention from human concerns to fix it elsewhere; it is, I would maintain, essential to meeting those concerns in a fully human way. As here entertained, however, God is not the invisible hand shaping events nor the Supreme quarterback calling all the plays. He is not to be looked to as the Source for specific directives or solutions. The working out of these is the task of human intelligence. Nor can God be called on to sanction the plans or programs we come up with. Neither issuing directives nor sanctioning complacency, God's presence continually, whatever our accomplishments, summons us to the task of intelligent action and calls all our achievements into question. It is the recognition of our responsibility to God, of the fact that intelligence is our responsive encounter with Being itself, that puts our whole life and all our deeds under judgment and prevents us from ever giving our final allegiance to anything finite, be it ourselves or the work of our hands. In God's presence we are never so just that we are not also sinners, never so sinful that the path to redeeming our past is closed. Thus, instead of being antagonistic to our humanity, God is its deliverer, its liberator. He frees us from the isolation of our own subjectivity while excluding our absorption by the collective. On the other hand, as judge of our collective efforts, he frees us from a slavery to our past, from thinking our communal structures to be any more than temporary improvisations in continual need of correction, from every ideology that would reduce our collective selves to a homogeneous mass, including those ideologies of intelligence, scientism and technologism.

Needless to say, God is all this for us only when the cultural embodiments of His presence allow Him to be so. Religion, as a cultural achievement, stands as much under God's judgment and is as continually in need of reform as anything else. That past religious traditions have not infrequently obscured God's liberating significance goes without saying. Nor is this the place for a discussion of how they might be revised. The point is that if God is really the One who frees man to build his world and become himself in the process, then there ar not a few, still standing, religous idols that must be tumbled to make room for Him. And if this is the case, then present-day atheism is not without positive religious import. By inconoclastically espousing the cause of human freedom and creativity, it has awakened the religious conscience from complacency to an ashamed awareness of its own shortcomings. Though not itself the full answer to man's plight nor a wholly reliable herald of salvation, nevertheless, by concentrating on the meaning of man it has thrown no little light on the meaning of God.

NOTES TO PART ONE

Works Referred to in This Part:

Blondel, Maurice, "Le point de départ de la recherche philosophique," *Annales de Philosophie Chrétienne,* 4ᵐᵉ Série, I (Octobre 1905–Mars 1906), 337–360; II (Avril–Septembre 1906), 225–249.

Bloy, Myron B., "The Christian Norm," in *Technology and Human Values.* The Fund for the Republic, 1966.

Callahan, Daniel, "The Secular City: Toward a Theology of Secularity," *Commonweal* LXXXII, 21 (September 17, 1965), 658–662.

cummings, e. e., *100 Selected Poems.* New York: 1959.

de Finance, Joseph, *Essai sur l'agir humain.* Rome: 1962.

Dewey, John, *Experience and Nature.* New York: 1958.

——, *On Experience, Nature and Freedom. Representative Selections,* ed. R. J. Bernstein. New York: 1960.

Fromm, Erich, *Escape from Freedom.* New York: 1960.

Guitton, Jean, *Essay on Human Love.* New York: 1951.

Macmurray, John, *The Self as Agent.* New York: 1957.

Niebuhr, H. Richard, *The Responsible Self.* New York: 1963.

Peirce, Charles Sanders, *Collected Papers,* eds. Charles Hartshorne, Paul Weiss, and Arthur Burks. 8 vols. Cambridge: 1931–58.

Pieper, Josef, *Leisure the Basis of Culture.* New York: 1952.

Scheler, Max, *Man's Place in Nature,* Hans Meyerhoff, trans. New York: 1962.

Page
14 Philosophy helps constitute life: Blondel, II, 241.
15 Need to set aside metaphysical worries: Callahan, 662.
16 "to step beyond . . . the workaday world." Pieper, 122.
16 "potentiality for consequences": *Experience and Nature,* 188.
17 "the place of science in life": *On Experience, Nature and Freedom,* 108.
17 "In a complicated and perverse world": *Ibid.,* 66.
18 "willing to turn away": *Experience and Nature,* 131.
21 "Some passionately held philosophy . . .": Bloy, 19.
21 "massive cultural shift": *Ibid.*
26 The controversy over contraceptive practices: *Catholic Mind* (January 1965), 2.
26 "It is not because reason is natural": de Finance, 306.
28 The norm of morality according to Aquinas: de Finance, 304–309.
29 "In regard to the greatest affairs of life": Peirce, 1.653.
31 Extracting an increase of being from suffering: Guitton, 180.
32 Unifying "subjectivity" and "objectivity": Fromm, 256–265.
32 "an affair of affairs": *Experience and Nature,* 97.
32 "the gay great happening": cummings, 114.
35 Universal scope and technical precision: Blondel, I, 337–9.
36 Philosophy cannot solve its old problems with its old methods: Macmurray, 17–38.
36 "wallow in metaphor": *Ibid.,* 28.
38 The brute animal "lives immersed in its environment": Scheler, 39.

38 Man's actions are "answers to actions upon him": Niebuhr, 64.
47 Philosophy's purpose not to explain life: Blondel, 11, 241.

NOTES TO PART TWO

Works Not Already Listed for Part One and Referred to in This Part:

Bolt, Robert, *A Man for All Seasons*. New York: 1962.
Collingwood, R. G., *The Idea of Nature*. New York: 1960.
Cox, Harvey, *The Secular City*. New York: 1965.
de Lubac, Henri, *The Drama of Atheist Humanism*. New York: 1950.
Dewey, John, *Art as Experience*. New York: 1934.
Fromm, Erich, *The Art of Loving*. New York: 1962.
Macmurray, John, *Persons in Relation*. London: 1961.
Maritain, Jacques, *The Rights of Man and the Natural Law*. New York: 1947.
Meany, John, "The Use of Authority," *America* (March 26, 1966), 409–411.
Perry, Ralph Barton, *The Thought and Character of William James*. 2 vols. Boston: 1935.
Rahner, Karl, "Christianity and Ideology," in *Concilium VI: The Church and the World*. New York: 1965.
Simon, Yves, *A General Theory of Authority*. Notre Dame: 1962.
Teilhard de Chardin, Pierre, *Letters from a Traveller*. New York: 1962.
———, *The Phenomenon of Man*. New York: 1959.
Tillich, Paul, *The Courage to Be*. New Haven: 1952.
———, *Love, Power, and Justice*. London: 1954.
Troisfontaines, Roger, *De l'existence à l'être: La philosophie de Gabriel Marcel*. 2 vols. Paris: 1953.
Wilhelmsen, Frederick D., *The Metaphysics of Love*. New York: 1962.

Page
58 "a conspirator with the sensual mind": *Art as Experience*, 31.
60 "Every encounter . . .": *Love, Power, and Justice*, 87.
62 Tradition and progress: Scheler, 26.
65 "image of man-the-answerer": Niebuhr, 56.
68 Man on the brink of nothingness: Scheler, 91.
70f. "If an historian": Collingwood, 25.
74 "only the sentimental face of love": *Phenomenon of Man*, 264.
75 "what being-*loved* makes being do": Wilhelmsen, 139.
78 Tillich on the self: *The Courage to Be*, 153–4.
80 Life is "a muddle and a struggle": William James, "Notebook," cited in Perry, 700.
81 "novelty and possibility forever leaking in": *Ibid*.
82 Man is "a community of persons": *Persons in Relation*, 12.
84 Citation of Simon: Meany, 409.
84 "The power in charge of unifying": Simon, 48.
84 Thomas More "became for me": Bolt, xii.
90 "the discovery by man that he has been left": Cox, 2.

90   "The epoch whose ethos is spreading": *Ibid.*, 3.

91   "Since this transcendence is not extrinsic": Rahner, 51.

91   "The true atheist is not the man": de Lubac, 11.

92   "As such, the collectivity is essentially unlovable": *Phenomenon of Man*, 267.

94   A Personal Other "who stands in the same mutual relation": *Persons in Relation*, 164.

96   "All meaningful knowledge": *The Self as Agent*, 16.

97   "that in our theories and in our acts": *Phenomenon of Man*, 257.

98   Marcel on *existence, objectification and being:* Troisfontaines, *passim.*

98   Fromm on the person's transcendence: *Art of Loving*, 7–9.

99   The person as open to the other: Scheler, 37–39.

99   Macmurray on science: *Persons in Relation*, 219–20.

99   The Scholastic view of man's vocation: Maritain, 60–61.

102   "a leap forward of the radial energies": *Phenomenon of Man*, 244.

102f.   advance "in a line continuous": *Ibid.*, 237.

103   "the natural confluence of grains of thought": *Ibid.*, 238.

104   Love alone "is capable of uniting living beings": *Ibid.*, 265.

104   "if there were no internal propensity to unite": *Ibid.*, 264.

105   "Love in all its subtleties": *Ibid.*, 265.

105   "Man's capacity, it may seem": *Ibid.*, 266.

105   "If the universe ahead of us": *Ibid.*, 267.

106   "charging itself at the very heart": *Ibid.*, n. 1.

106   "who stands in the same mutual relation": *Persons in Relation*, 164.

108   Tillich on love and power: *Love, Power, and Justice*, 49.

113   "The longer I live": *Letters from a Traveller*, 160.

NOTES TO PART THREE

Works Not Already Listed for Parts One and Two and Referred to in This Part:

Clarke, Norris, "Is the West 'God's Civilization'?" *America* (March 31, 1962), 853–856.

de Finance, Joseph, "Being and Subjectivity," *Cross Currents* VI, 2 (Spring 1956), 163–178.

Dewey, John, *A Common Faith*. New Haven: 1934.

———, *The Quest for Certainty*. New York: 1929.

Dewey and Tufts, *Ethics*. New York: 1932.

Hook, Sidney, "Neither Blind Obedience nor Uncivil Disobedience," *New York Times Magazine* (June 5, 1966), 52–3+.

Johann, Robert O., *The Pragmatic Meaning of God*. Milwaukee: 1966.

Lacroix, Jean, *The Meaning of Modern Atheism*. Dublin: 1965.

Milhaven, John Giles, "Be like me! Be Free!" *America* (April 22, 1967), 584–586.

Mounier, Emmanuel, *The Character of Man*. New York: 1956.

O'Connor, D. J., *An Introduction to the Philosophy of Education*. New York: 1957.

Pieper, Josef, *Justice*. New York: 1955.

Weil, Simone, *Selected Essays 1934–43*. New York: 1962.

Vahanian, G., *The Death of God*. New York: 1957.

————, "Swallowed up by Godlessness," *The Christian Century* (December 8, 1965), 1505–1507.

Wheelis, Allen, *The Quest for Identity*. New York: 1958.

Page

119   Bertrand Russell on the reasonable man: O'Connor, 27.

120   No philosophy except in religious context: *Leisure the Basis of Culture,* 147–166.

124   "Reality is not delivered to your door": Mounier, 105.

130   "Essential as the presence of others is for us": "Being and Subjectivity," 174.

130   Not man-the-maker, nor man-the-citizen: Niebuhr, 49–65.

135   The chaos in civic life: Hook, *passim*.

137   "If you say to someone": Weil, 21.

137   "Man has inalienable rights": *Justice,* 21.

138   "Justice is something that comes second": *Ibid.,* 13.

143   He "in so far commits himself": *Ethics,* 182.

146   "As a matter of fact, they weren't that free": Milhaven, 586.

154   "ultimate values are matters of extrarational personal preference": Clarke, 854.

155   "let us first examine the facts": Wheelis, 73.

155   Bertrand Russell on the rational man: O'Connor, 27.

157   Marcel on *subject* and *object:* Troisfontaines, I, 77–80.

170   Man must first fill his life with reality: Blondel, II, 239.

171   Atheism as a starting-point: Lacroix, 8.

171   The death of God as cultural event: Vahanian, *passim.*

173   Not atheism vs. theism, but idolatry vs. iconoclasm: "Swallowed up by Godlessness," 1507.

176   "The old center was mind": *The Quest for Certainty,* 290–291.

176f. Erich Fromm on the great problem of today: *Escape from Freedom,* 256–265.

178   "as a snail carries its shell": Scheler, 39.

179f. "Since this transcendence": Rahner, 51.

182   The primary locus of Christianity: *Ibid.,* 50.

182   "advocates a program": *Ibid.,* 43.

182   "These objectivizations": *Ibid.,* 45.

184   "faith in the methods of intelligence": *A Common Faith,* 87.

186   Community as a response to initiative: Johann, 50–54.

186   Vahanian on the present-day ethic: *The Death of God,* 193.